LibrarySparks™

Library Lessons

A collection of the finest Library Lessons from *LibrarySparks* Magazine

Edited by Diane Findlay

UpstartBooks™

Madison, Wisconsin

Published by UpstartBooks
4810 Forest Run Road
Madison, WI 53704

1-800-448-4887

Table of Contents

Introduction

When my editor at Upstart approached me about working with a compendium of library lessons from the first six volumes of *LibrarySparks,* I was delighted. Not only is it fun to wear a compiler/editor's hat for a change, but I love *LibrarySparks!* I look forward to finding it in my mailbox each month, and I mine it for the many gems that are always there to be found. Since I write for the magazine, I know what's coming in terms of themes and features, which heightens my eagerness to explore the great ideas and resources other writers bring to subjects that are much on my mind.

The lessons you'll find here are written by creative, talented front-line educators whose work blends first-rate professional know-how with that special gift of being tuned in to the interests of kids and the standards-driven needs of teachers. The lessons span the calendar from library orientation to promoting summer reading, cover a wide range of content from apples and pumpkins to poetry, and incorporate methods and tools from the timeless appeal of puppets to PowerPoint and online reference sources. In choosing among the many great lessons available, I tried to balance that range of content and methods with lessons at different grade levels, written by different authors, that exercise different critical thinking skills and engage different intelligences and learning styles. I've updated the lessons and resources as needed so that, at the time of this writing, all books are in print and all websites up and running.

Whether you're a highly experienced veteran or a rookie bursting with enthusiasm, you'll find something useful here. Use the lessons "as is" or let them spark creative adaptations to suit your unique situation. May your library lessons be inspired and may your students look forward to library day with bright anticipation!

Diane Findlay

Contributors

- **Sharron Cohen** is a former Bookmobile librarian at the Sawyer Free Library in Gloucester, Massachusetts. She is the author of *The Mysteries of Research, Second Edition* and *The Mysteries of Internet Research* from UpstartBooks.

- **Diane Findlay** has worked with children's and young adult literature for more than twenty-five years and was the director of the Waukee (Iowa) Public Library for six years. She is the author of the Exploring Children's Literature series and *Digging Into Dewey* from UpstartBooks.

- **Nancy Riemer Kellner**, a longtime *LibrarySparks* reviewer, is enjoying her twelfth year as the librarian (or "library teacher" as she prefers to be called) at the Marguerite E. Peaslee Elementary School in Northborough, Massachusetts.

- **Aileen Kirkham** is the author of *Library Lessons for Little Ones*, the intermediate Collaborative Bridges series (both from UpstartBooks), and articles for *Library Media Connection* and *LibrarySparks*. She is also an educational consultant for professional development, a library media specialist at Decker Prairie Elementary in the Tomball Independent School District, and a professional storyteller and puppeteer. Visit Aileen's website at www.aileenkirkham.com.

- **Gloria Koster** is an elementary library media specialist at West School in New Canaan, Connecticut. She is the author of *The Peanut-Free Café* from Albert Whitman.

- **Debra LaPlante** is a teacher-librarian and district library coordinator in the Alhambra School District in Phoenix, Arizona, and serves as co-director of the Central Arizona Writing Project.

- **Karen Larsen** is a teacher-librarian at Cotton Creek Elementary School in Westminster, Colorado. She is the author of *Careers!* from ALPS Publishing, the co-author of *State by State* from Pieces of Learning, and the co-author of

Day by Day: Professional Journaling for Library Media Specialists, from Linworth. Karen is a frequent contributor to *LibrarySparks*.

- **Pat Miller** is a career library media specialist. She is author of *Squirrel's New Year's Resolution* from Albert Whitman; the Stretchy Lesson Plan series, the Stretchy Library Lessons series, and *We're Going on a Book Hunt* from UpstartBooks; as well as *Reaching Every Reader* from Linworth. Visit her website at www.patmillerbooks.com.

- **Judith Snyder** is a seasoned teacher-librarian in Colorado, as well as a professional storyteller and freelance writer. Judith is the author of the Jump-start Your Library series from UpstartBooks, and two picture books, *What Do You See?* and *Stinky Feet* from Odyssey Books. Visit her website at www.judithsnyderwrites.com for additional literacy ideas and articles featuring integration of the arts and creative thinking.

- **Lynne Farrell Stover** has more than thirty years of experience as an educator and is currently a teacher consultant at James Madison University in Harrisonburg, Virginia. She has taught many teacher workshops and won Teacher of the Year in 1999 from the Virginia Council of Economic Education and from the Virginia Association for the Gifted. She is the author of *Magical Library Lessons*, *More Magical Library Lessons*, *Magical Library Lessons: Holiday Happenings*, and *From Snicket to Shakespeare* from UpstartBooks.

Welcome Home

• Library Lessons •

by | Pat Miller

W elcome to a new year in the library! You may have some energetic new ideas, booktalks for new books you read this summer, and perhaps a new puppet or prop for a lesson you want to try. But first you have to plan your library orientation lessons. The word "orientation" originally meant to arrange in reference to the east. Now it means to introduce a new situation and help people adapt to it.

Orientation is the way we acquaint students with our policies, procedures, and the physical arrangement of our library, whether it faces east or not! We want students to feel comfortable with the hows and wheres of our library. Our goal is to make them productive, independent library users.

More importantly for students, starting school means finding their place in their peer group. Some students will be new to the class or the school and will feel anxious. You can alleviate their discomfort when you meet your classes for the first time. Design orientation activities so students become acquainted with resources and each other and have some fun. If you do, the library will rank high on students' lists of places they want to be.

Library Survivor | Grades 3–5

Objective

To get acquainted with one another and with the library.

Supplies

- a plastic lei for each player (each team should have a different color). Get them from a local party store or Oriental Trading Company (www.orientaltrading.com).
- destination markers (palm tree pattern on page 10)
- shells (available at a local hobby store)
- permanent black marker
- decorated clue scroll for each team (scroll pattern on page 10)
- adhesive name tags
- fine-tipped black markers

Prepare in Advance

- Prepare a list of library sites you want the students to locate (e.g., fiction, circulation desk, PAC computers, etc.). Photocopy the list for each team.

- Photocopy a palm tree for each site. Number the palm trees so they correspond with your list.

- Place the appropriate palm tree marker at each site. Surround the marker with one shell for each team. Write the site number on each shell in black marker.

- Photocopy the scroll, and write a list of questions about library policies and procedures on it. For example: How long can we keep our library books? What is the fine for overdue books? Photocopy a scroll for each team. Roll up the scrolls and tie them with raffia or twine. Attach a feather or tiny beads if you like. This will become their "tree mail."

To Play

1. Form teams with a mix of boys and girls, new and former students and students from various homerooms from the previous year. Each team should have four or five players.

2. Have the teams introduce themselves to each other and don their team leis. Distribute name tags and ask the children to write their first names in large letters on the tags before wearing.

3. Hand out the numbered list of sites to each team.

4. Teams should locate each site. At each destination they should explain its usage to one another and any new students on their team. When they have finished they should collect a shell, then move on to the next destination.

5. Teams should visit as many sites and collect as many shells as possible within a stated time limit.

6. When the time is up, pass out each team's "tree mail" and give them a short amount of time to talk over answers to the questions.

7. Gather the teams in a central area and ask them questions from the scroll. Take turns calling on random students from each team. Each correct answer earns a point for the team, as does each collected shell.

To Win

The team with the most points wins the game. Let them check out an additional book or pass out a small prize to each team member.

Good Books, Good Friends | Grade K–2

Objective

To learn the policies and procedures of the library.

Note: The first week with younger classes I explain the areas for checkout, how to access their library cards, how to check out books, and how to hug a book with a gentle bear hug. I send a parent letter home with a sign (see sample on page 11) suitable for attaching to the refrigerator to remind the family of the child's library day. In later classes I cover book care, returning books on time, etc. Each week I review policies from the previous week and add a few more until all have been explained. It is easy to overwhelm young students in your big exciting library!

Supplies

- checklist of areas and policies to explain
- adhesive name tags
- fine-tipped black markers
- copies of parent letter from page 11

Prepare in Advance

- Decorate your library in a colorful and friendly manner. This might include book posters, stuffed book characters ,and books faced front and placed in low baskets.

- Write each student's name in large letters on a name tag.

- Fill out the parent letter. Make a photocopy for each student.

To Play

1. Pass out name tags and have students wear them.

2. Have each student pick a partner. If the group is an odd number, let one group have three students.

3. Explain and demonstrate your library policies.

4. Allow student pairs to select two books, with each student choosing a book for his or her partner. To choose well, students will have to ask questions to find out about their partner's interests. Explain that it is like choosing a present for their partners.

To Win

Each student will have found interesting books and possibly a new friend.

Know Your Reader | Grades 3–5

Note: If you have an orientation procedure, perhaps you can add a get-acquainted game before or after your library introduction.

Objective

To get acquainted with students while discussing reading habits.

Supplies

- a pencil for each student
- Know Your Reader game card (see page 12)
- a clipboard or cardboard backing sheet for each student
- adhesive name tags
- fine-tipped black markers

Prepare in Advance

- Sharpen a class set of pencils.
- Photocopy a Know Your Reader game card for each student.

To Play

1. Before the game, introduce yourself and describe some of your reading habits, including something you read and enjoyed recently.

2. Distribute name tags and ask children to write their first names in large letters on the tags before wearing.

3. Pass out a game card to each student. Read aloud the categories so students have a chance to hear them and decide which apply to them. Most will be able to sign their name in several boxes.

4. Have students mingle and get acquainted by gathering signatures (first names only) of class-mates in an effort to make tic-tac-toe. There should be only one name in each box.

5. To extend the time and encourage more interaction, have students go beyond tic-tac-toe and collect as many signatures as there are students in class (or twenty-five, whichever is less).

6. This is not a race, but it is a timed activity. Encourage students to take their time and get acquainted as they gather signatures.

7. If you like, reread the categories after the game and ask for a show of hands of students who fit each category.

To Win

Everyone who gets tic-tac-toe can check out an extra book or go to the shelves first.

For an alternate activity for grades K–2, see page 13.

Additional Resources

- **57 Games to Play in the Library or Classroom** by Carol K. Lee and Fay Edwards. Alleyside Press, 1997. Includes orientation games called "Glad Book, Sad Book," "Media Manners" and "Media Center Alphabet."

- **Fun-Brarian: Games, Activities & Ideas to Liven Up Your Library!** by Kathleen Fox. UpstartBooks, 2007.

- **Instant Library Lessons** series by Karen A. Farmer Wanamaker. UpstartBooks.

- **Library Mania** by Charlene C. Cali. UpstartBooks, 2008.

- **Stretchy Library Lessons** series by Pat Miller. UpstartBooks. *Library Skills* title includes detailed orientation lessons called "Where in the Library" and "I Spy."

Date: _____

Dear Parents:

Today your child came to our school library for the first time. He/she is bringing home _____ books.

They are due back to the library on your child's library day, which is _____.

Please help us encourage good habits in these areas:

- How to handle books carefully;
- How to keep books in a safe place;
- How to return books to the library on time.

In our library, we do not charge fines for late books. However, we do charge for book damages. Charges may include replacing the book. If the book is lost, we charge the cost to replace the book.

I look forward to sharing my love of reading and books with your child. If you have questions, please call.

Sincerely,

_____ (Name)

_____ (Phone)

My Library Day is

_____

Please hang this on your refrigerator where it will be seen.

Know Your Reader

Go around the room and get to know your classmates. Find someone who fits the description in each box. Have that person write his or her first name in the box. There should only be one name in each box. Try to get tic-tac-toe.

prefers mysteries	read for a summer reading program	reads before going to sleep	has made something by following the directions	owns at least ten books
read a book and saw the movie	buys from the class book order	got a book for a gift	bought a book from a bookstore	had an overdue book
read all of the Harry Potter books	reads the newspaper	has parents who like to read	has done a book report	has watched *Reading Rainbow*
likes *Charlotte's Web*	won a prize for reading	likes nonfiction better than fiction	prefers paperbacks to hardcover books	enjoys stories read aloud
gets a magazine subscription at home	reads the cereal box during breakfast	shops at the school book fair	reads books by the same author	reads comic books

Step Up, Readers!

Alternate activity for grades K–2

If your library has space, play this game with younger students as an alternate to "Know Your Reader." Have all students stand along a taped start line. The caller—you or an aide, volunteer, or designated student—should stand opposite the class, behind a taped line. As the caller reads each statement below, those who agree take a step forward. As the students cross the finish line, they can check out books. When you get down to five who haven't crossed the line, stop the game and allow them to check out as well.

★ Reads before going to sleep

★ Has made something by following the directions

★ Owns at least ten books

★ Read a book and saw the movie

★ Buys from the class book order

★ Got a book for a gift

★ Bought a book from a bookstore

★ Had an overdue book

★ Read several of Marc Brown's Arthur books

★ Prefers mysteries

★ Read for a summer reading program

★ Reads the comics in the newspaper

★ Has parents who like to read

★ Has done a book report

★ Watches *Reading Rainbow*

★ Likes Clifford books

★ Won a prize for reading

★ Likes nonfiction better than fiction

★ Prefers paperbacks to hardcover books

★ Enjoys stories read aloud

★ Gets a magazine subscription at home

★ Reads the cereal box during breakfast

★ Shops at the school book fair

★ Reads books by the same author

★ Reads comic books

Library Orientation 101

by | Aileen Kirkham   **Grades PK–2, 3–5**

Welcome students to a new year in the library by giving a library orientation lesson. Depending on students' ages, orientation may take several visits to complete. Invite your students to be seated; then use a puppet to introduce the lesson. I use a large, full-body, sheepdog puppet from Folkmanis that I've named Kitty. I keep the puppet hidden until everyone is seated. Then I look for him by calling his name. Before I display Kitty, he barks. The students wonder why I've been calling a kitty that barks. (Humor is essential for library instruction.) Kitty comes out of hiding and introduces himself. He tells the students that he got his name from a very good book—A Dog Called Kitty by Bill Wallace (Simon & Schuster, 1992). Then Kitty does a chant to promote reading.

"Kitty's Reading Chant"
Reading—it is doggone great, because of this we celebrate.
A special story we'll share this day, give a shout—Hip! Hip! Hooray!
Reading—it is doggone great. (Position puppet to howl this final phrase.)

Encourage Kitty to introduce the librarian and other library personnel. Ask Kitty if he'd like to stay for the story. Kitty is eager. Seat him out of the students' reach, where they can see him. Read aloud the grade-appropriate story below. As you read, emphasize tips about book care that occur in the story.

Stories to Share

Pre-Kindergarten and Kindergarten
I. Q. Goes to the Library by Mary Ann Fraser.
Walker & Company, 2003.

Introduce the story by singing the following song to a mouse puppet.

(Sung to the tune: "Heigh-ho" from Snow White and the Seven Dwarfs)
I. Q., I. Q. a very smart mouse are you,
You go to school and read books, too,
I. Q., I. Q.-I.Q.-I.Q.

Greet the mouse puppet, "I. Q., we're so glad you came to share your story today." Have the mouse whisper in your ear and respond by saying, "Yes, I.

Q., the boys and girls are going to learn how to get books from the library today." Read *I. Q. Goes to the Library* and discuss the story. Display a library card like I. Q.'s and explain its purpose. Discuss why book care at home and at school is necessary so I. Q. and all the boys and girls at school can take turns reading and enjoying the books all year long.

First Grade
Book! Book! Book!
by Deborah Bruss.
Scholastic, 2001.

This book lends
itself very well to
student participa-
tion. Introduce the
book by making a
hen's clucking sound. Have the students guess which
animal on the farm makes that noise. Then tell them
that when you cup your hand to your ear, it is their
cue to repeat an animal sound. Do this throughout
the story; the children will anxiously await their cues
to help tell the story with a variety of animal sounds.
Discuss book care at home and at school. Tell the
students what their responsibility is if a book is damaged or lost.

Second Grade
*The Librarian
from the Black
Lagoon* by Mike
Thaler. Scholastic,
2008.

Introduce the
story with this
song.

"The Librarian of the Black Lagoon"
(Sung to the tune: "The Ants Go Marching")

The Librarian of the Black Lagoon,
she's watching you.
The Librarian of the Black Lagoon,
she's watching you.
The Librarian of the Black Lagoon,
if you don't watch out,
She'll pounce on you, but not if you obey the
rules of the library.

Read the story aloud. Discuss the humor and why the
author used a scary character to introduce kids to the
library. (It's a fun place to be and welcomes all kids,
but there are important rules that are necessary for all
to enjoy the library.) Discuss the book care rules in
your library.

Third Grade
Library Lil by Suzanne
Williams. Dial, 1997.

As you share this story, have
students become actors.
When you pause during the
reading, give them an adjective to describe the character
or use one that is in the story.
For example, for "surly," model a rude or unfriendly
attitude for the students, then let them do it. Another
enhancement for this story is for the reader to use a
variety of voices for the characters. For example: Bill's
voice could be deep, raspy, and harsh. Discuss the
story; then review the rules of good book care.

Fourth and Fifth Grades
The Library Dragon
by Carmen Agra Deedy.
Peachtree Publishers, 1994.

As you share this story, cue
students to do a repetitive
refrain of "Smoking!" when
the library dragon gets mad or
burns something. As a signal,
cup your hand to your ear.
This book, too, lends itself to
using a variety of voices. For
example, mean and nasty for

the Library Dragon, but changing to sweet and kind
when she becomes the Library Goddess. Discuss the
story; then review the rules of good book care.

Library Tour

Lead a tour of the library facilities and define the
purpose of each. In my library, we tour:

- Story Room/Theater—where stories are shared

- Student Stations—a bank of computers for student use

- Reference Area—tables, chairs, reference books,
  AV presentation equipment, etc. (Books in this
  area are for in-library use only or for classroom
  checkout by the teachers.)

The Everybody Books at the Rosehill Elementary School library.

- Leisure Reading Area—kid-friendly chairs and cushions with a magazine rack; an area where students read until the entire class has finished selection and checkout
- Stacks
- Bilingual Library—special collection for kids lucky enough to read and speak two languages (This is a terrific opportunity to share the fact that kids who learn two or more languages will have more opportunities in our global society.)
- Everybody Books/Picture Books
- Fiction Books
- Nonfiction
- Professional Library—for staff members only

Magnificent Library Manners

Post your library rules in a highly visible place. Point out and discuss the rules. It helps if students understand the rationales for the rules. Tell the students that the rules will be posted all year, to help them remember. An excellent location for posting the rules is by the library doors. The following are examples of rules in my library:

- Use a 6" voice. Use a ruler to show students how long 6" is, and remind them that their voices should not stretch beyond that distance.
- Respect other students working in the library; do not visit with them.
- Push in your chairs so your neighbors won't trip over them.

- Treat all library materials with care. Tell children that many students and staff members will share the same library materials this year.
- Return magazines and reference materials to their original locations.
- Bring a library card and pass when coming individually to the library. Clothespins make inexpensive passes. Write the teacher's last name on one side and "Library" on the other side. We issue two library passes per classroom for grades 1–4.
- Do not move furniture without permission.
- Take turns if you need to share materials.
- Use a shelf marker when searching for books. Demonstrate how the shelf marker holds the spot where the book lives.
- Bring your books back on time. Tell students how long they can keep the books and what your renewal policies are.

Checking Out Books

Give your students specific instructions on how to check out books. Point them to each location in the order necessary to complete the process. To reinforce understanding, have them point and recite the order. Some students will remember the process from last year, but it helps to review. Other students are new and may not have seen this process in action.

To check out a book:
- Get your shelf marker.
- Find your book(s).
- Get your card.

- Put your shelf marker back.
- Check out your book(s).
- Sit down and read.

Staff Orientation Tips

Prior to the start of the new school year, visit with your principal and schedule a time for staff library orientation. This should take place before the first day with students. My principal implemented a terrific plan which provides a half day of staff development for a rotation where the faculty is divided into three groups. They travel to three locations: administrative procedures with front office staff, library in-service with library staff, and special subjects/special programs with PE, Art, Music, Computer Lab, Special Ed, etc.

At the library orientation session, try an introductory skit. One of my favorites is to use magician props of a hat and a wand. After waving the wand over the hat, I pull out a snack size bag of M&M's. Then I announce "TA DA! The letters stand for Media Magicians and that's what the library staff wants you to know. We provide the magic of supporting the curriculum through programming and services. And our service is "M-M Good!" Pass out snack size M&M's to all staff members.

I also pass out library handbooks. You can use pocket folders with labels, but I prefer notebooks that are labeled and barcoded as part of the professional book collection. They can be returned at the end of the school year and updated each year. Inside the handbook include a memo on standard procedures; services; programming dates for special events such as book fairs and guest speakers; deadlines for grade levels to submit unit outlines to assist with collection development; and the schedules for library lessons and group checkout. Review highlights of the memo and ask staff members to read it. Direct them to keep the handbook as a handy reference guide and for filing future library memos. You may also wish to include the database listing of supplemental reading programs such as Accelerated Reader or Reading Counts. This provides students and teachers with a list that is readily accessible for labeling classroom library books and checking reading levels of books from home and public libraries.

Take the group on a tour of the library. Emphasize the locations of professional media: read-aloud kits, puppet collection, big books, videos, DVDs, professional books collection, etc.

In the same session or as a follow-up, schedule time for hands-on training on library software, especially the automated catalog for requesting library materials.

Library Town

• Library Lessons •

by | Gloria Koster

Community is often a unit of study in the primary grades. Beginning with "myself" and "my family," students learn that both "my class" and "my school" are communities. They may visit important places in their town and meet community workers. The world expands for young children as they are introduced to states, countries, and continents, and they become familiar with maps and globes.

You can capitalize on primary grade units that deal with community to explain and simplify library organization. Call numbers are like addresses. Library books are located on shelves in the same way that houses are located on streets. Fiction and nonfiction sections are like two separate neighborhoods, and finding your way around any library or accessing information from a specific book is not so different from navigating in the real world. Recognizing, interpreting, and using guideposts are the themes of this Library Town unit.

Lesson 1: Addresses and Call Numbers

Materials

- *Me on the Map* by Joan Sweeney (Crown Publishers, 1996)

- *From Here to There* by Margery Cuyler (Henry Holt & Company, 1999)

- transparency of Library Town Map (see page 21)

- map of your town

- squares of lined paper

- copy of House Pattern for each student (see page 22)

- yarn

Concepts

- A library is like a town.

- In a town there are streets with buildings; in the library there are shelves with books.

- Each building in a town has an address; each book in the library has a call number.

Lesson

1. Read *Me on the Map* and *From Here to There*.

2. Compare the illustrations on the opening pages of the books. Where is the main character in the beginning of each book? What other places are depicted in both books? What's the name for a drawing of a place that shows where things are?

3. Show a map of the town in which the students live. Ask students what we will need to know in order to place their homes on the map. (*Street names and addresses*)

4. Use an overhead projector to show the Library Town Map. How will we know where to place different books on the "library streets"? Discuss the fact that books, like houses, have addresses. These addresses are called call numbers. They appear on the spines of books.

Activity

1. Have each student write his or her name and address on a square of lined paper. Supply younger students with address information as needed.

2. Hand out copies of the House Pattern. Students will cut out the house and paste the address information on the front.

3. Have students decorate their houses.

4. Attach the houses around the map of your town with yarn connecting each house to the appropriate street on the map.

Closing

- Review terms: "map," "address," "call number."

- Ask, "When I walk down your street, where will I see your address?" (mailbox, signpost, wall)

- Ask, "When I walk down a street in Library Town, where will I see the 'addresses?' What are these book addresses called?"

Lesson 2: Neighborhoods for Books

Materials

- *The Village of Round and Square Houses* by Ann Grifalconi (Little, Brown and Company, 1986)

- Town map with student houses (from Lesson One)

- Library Town Map transparency (from Lesson One)

- transparency marker

- several slips of paper with call numbers written on them

Lesson

1. Read *The Village of Round and Square Houses*. Ask, "If all library books could be placed in just two types of houses, what would the two categories be?" Establish that fiction and nonfiction are the two umbrella categories for books.

2. Display the Library Town Map on an overhead projector. With a transparency marker, fill in some call numbers on the spines of books in different sections. Ask students why some call numbers have letters on top and others have numbers. Students may be able to determine that some books are fiction and some are nonfiction.

3. Ask why the nonfiction books have so many different numbers. Explain that the numbers are connected to what the book is about (the subject). Books live in subject "neighborhoods."

4. Have students focus on the second line of information on the call numbers. Does the second line contain letters or numbers? Once students realize that the second line of information contains letters, introduce author letters.

5. With a transparency marker, fill in the top line of several more call numbers, asking whether the numbers represent fiction or nonfiction.

6. Ask for student volunteers. Students will pretend that they are authors and complete the call numbers, using their own last names for the author letters.

Closing

- How is a library like the village of round and square houses?

- What are the two big neighborhoods in any library? Invite a few students to come up individually and decide the correct neighborhood and street (shelf) for call numbers that you have written on slips of paper.

Lesson 3: Locating What You Need

Materials

- *Where's Pup?* by Dayle Ann Dodds (Dial, 2003)
- transparencies of one table of contents page and one index from any book
- Build a Table of Contents (see page 23)
- Build an Index (see page 24)

Concepts

- In towns and libraries certain people can help you find what you are looking for. Towns and libraries both have helpful signs and guideposts.
- Guideposts in libraries can help you find a book.
- Guideposts in a book can help you find specific information.
- An index and a table of contents are two types of guideposts that you will find in many books.

Lesson

1. Read *Where's Pup?* Discuss these questions: What is the circus clown's problem? How does he try to solve the problem of his missing dog? If you were missing something in town, how could you solve your problem? Who would you ask? What else could you do? If you could not find a book in the library, who might you ask for help? What else could you do to find the book?

2. Once you have the book, how can you find the information you need? What guides do many books have to help you?

3. Project an image of a table of contents. What is this list called? Where in the book is it found? In what order are the chapters listed?

4. Project an image of an index. What is this list called? Where in the book is it found? In what order are the words of the index listed?

Activity

1. Divide the class in half.

2. Have the first group cut out chapter headings and numbers from Build a Table of Contents, and paste them appropriately on a piece of blank paper to create a table of contents. While chapter headings may be in any order that makes sense to the group, page numbers must appear in increasing numerical order.

3. Have the second group cut out words and numbers from Build an Index and paste them appropriately on a blank piece of paper to create an index. While the index key words must be in alphabetical order, there is no right order for the page numbers, since they refer to pages in a nonexistent text.

Closing

- Review using these prompts: What are two ways that we can get information from a book without reading the whole thing?
- How are a contents page and index arranged differently?
- When the class leaves the library, have them line up in "index" order according to their last names.

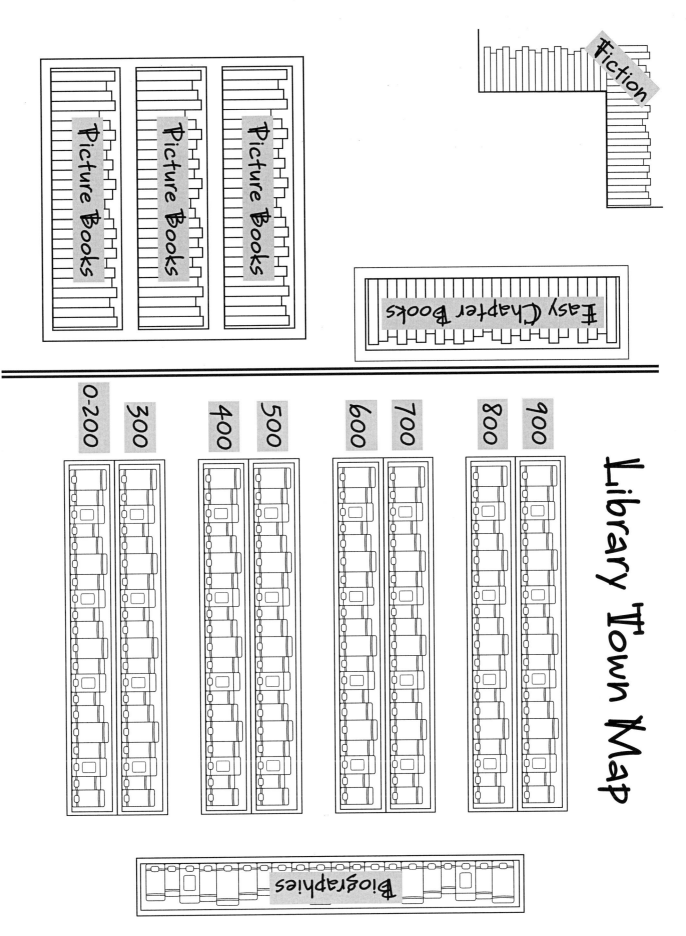

Library Town Map

House Pattern

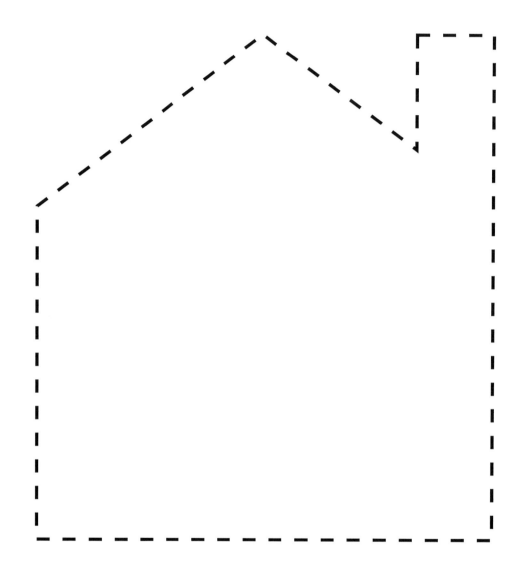

Build a Table of Contents

Meet the Frog

Where Frogs Live

What Frogs Eat

Frog Friends

Frog Enemies

Funny Frog Facts

1

4

7

12

16

20

Build an Index

Bear

Zebra

Penguin

Deer

Rooster

Anteater

3

14

15

7

30

5

Apples, Pumpkins, Research!

• Library Lessons •

by | Pat Miller

Think October and you probably think Halloween. Pumpkins or jack-o'-lanterns may be your next thought. October is the peak month for harvesting pumpkins and apples, and it is a great time to interest students in a variety of research opportunities using these fruits.

Because it is still early in the school year, you may not have had time to introduce the variety of research sources in your library. Consider a series of short lessons based on questions about this October produce, and introduce some fun at the same time. Before beginning, you may want to purchase a selection of pumpkins and apples to display next to labeled tent cards. Along with the fresh fruit, you might include pumpkin and apple products.

The research tools used in the following activities are:

- dictionary
- almanac
- atlas
- general encyclopedia, plant encyclopedia, or on-line encyclopedia
- Internet
- nonfiction books

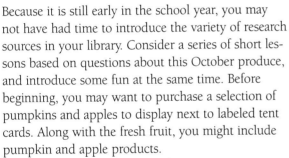

Set up learning centers for each of the resources, and copy the questions for each resource on a 3" x 5" task card to laminate. Put the task card in a 4" x 6" manila envelope. On the front, add a picture of an apple, pumpkin, or both. Alternatively, you could write the task questions on strips of paper and put them inside a plastic jack-o'-lantern.

Each resource center will need:

- task card(s)
- pencil and paper for each student
- the appropriate research tool

Review the resources with your students as needed, then divide children into six groups. Assign each group a starting resource center. The groups should move around the library, completing each center as they go. You will be stationed at the Nonfiction Books resource center. Monitor students' progress as they work.

Dictionary

Tasks

1. What word did "pumpkin" come from?

2. Is a pumpkin a fruit or a vegetable?

3. Besides its color, what else does the definition tell you about a pumpkin?

4. Define "apple."

5. Besides the definition, what other information does the dictionary supply about an apple?

Almanac

Tasks

1. Which states grow pumpkins to sell commercially?

2. Which states are major apple producers?

3. List five pumpkin-producing states and five apple-producing states on a sheet of paper. Locate the population for each state. Then number each group of five in order of their size, from smallest to largest.

4. What similarities do you notice about the weather in the pumpkin- or apple-producing states? What does this tell you about the kind of weather needed to grow pumpkins and apples?

Atlas

Photocopy the "Atlas Research" worksheet from page 28 for each student. Have a pile of worksheets at the resource center.

Tasks

1. Use the atlas and worksheet to locate the major pumpkin-producing states. Next to each, record the latitude and longitude of its capital city.

2. Use the atlas and worksheet to locate the major apple-producing states. Next to each, record the latitude and longitude of its capital city.

Encyclopedia

Photocopy the "Pumpkins: True or False?" worksheet from page 29 for each student. Have a pile of worksheets at the resource center.

Task

Use the encyclopedia to answer the questions on the worksheet. Record the page number where you found each fact.
Answers:
False: 3, 6, 8, 10.
True: 1, 2, 4, 5, 7, 9.

Internet

Premier Star Company has a site called "Pumpkin Recipes Galore" and they are not exaggerating! Go to www.pumpkinnook.com/cook book.htm to find forty-six recipes for dishes like pumpkin pie, cake, cookies, chili, ice cream, dip, milk shake, and even seven international recipes including Moroccan Pumpkin Soup and Italian Pumpkin Marmalade. Have students visit this site or find apple and/or pumpkin recipes in your cookbook collection.

Tasks

1. Record the names of three pumpkin or apple recipes and the fractions used in each.

2. Which fraction is used most often? Why don't you see a fraction like $^{11}/_{16}$ of a cup?

3. Which recipe would you like to make? Why?

Additional Internet Research:
Have students visit the University of Illinois Extension site, www.urbanext.uiuc.edu/pump kins/history.html for information on carving and displaying pumpkins.

Tasks

1. What was the original "Jack O'Lantern" made from?

2. How did the custom of carving faces into fruits or vegetables begin?

Nonfiction Books

Listening to or reading nonfiction books is more challenging than reading fiction. Students often miss information because they use the same reading speed and level of attention they do with "chapter books." At this resource center you will read aloud a nonfiction book about pumpkins or apples. Before class, choose an appropriate book and develop five to ten questions from it. You may also use the sample questions below. Get students' ears ready for your book by asking the questions and recording the groups' three best guesses. Or read a question and three answers. Ask students to hold up one finger for

"A," two for "B," and three for "C." Do not tell the answers. Then read the book aloud. Students will listen for details, if only to see if their guess was correct.

Tasks
Sample Questions

Note: These sample questions can be answered using books from the bibliography. If you are reading a specific title aloud, ask questions in the order that students will hear the answers. Include some questions that students should be able to answer using prior knowledge. This assures that all will get at least one answer correct.

1. How many seeds do apples have?

    A) five   B) six   C) seven

2. How many kinds of apples are there in the world?

    A) 350   B) 1,000   C) 7,500

3. How many apples are picked by hand in the United States each fall?

    A) none, machines do it   B) 3 million
    C) 3 billion

4. How big was the largest recorded pumpkin?

    A) 30 pounds   B) about 250 pounds
    C) Over 1,000 pounds

5. What percentage of a pumpkin is water?

    A) 90%   B) 50%   C) 25%

6. How many calories are in an average-sized apple?

    A) 350 calories   B) 20 calories
    C) 80 calories

7. How long ago were apples first grown as a food crop?

    A) 1,000 years ago   B) 3,000 years ago
    C) 5,000 years ago

Answers:
1) a, 2) c, 3) c, 4) b, 5) a, 6) c, 7) b

Apple Matching

If you have time, set up one additional resource center with a book from your collection that identifies apple varieties by name, such as *Apples* by Gail Gibbons. Buy as many matching apples as you can find. Set them up in a numbered display. Have a pile of answer sheets at the resource center. Once everyone has completed this station, enter all answer sheets that have at least two correct answers in a drawing. The prizes might be an apple, an individually wrapped fried apple pie, applesauce, apple juice, or apple chews.

Task

Examine the apples and the pictures in the book. Complete the answer sheet. (For a sample answer sheet, see page 30.)

Pumpkin and Apple Books

- *The Apple Pie Tree* by Zoe Hall. Scholastic, 1996.

- *Apples* by Gail Gibbons. Holiday House, 2001.

- *Apples and Pumpkins* by Anne Rockwell. Simon & Schuster, 1994.

- *Apples of Your Eye* by Allan Fowler. Children's Press, 1994.

- *Apple Trees* by Gail Saunders-Smith. Pebble Books, 1998.

- *Eating Apples* by Gail Saunders-Smith. Pebble Books, 1998.

- *How Do Apples Grow?* by Betsy Maestro. HarperCollins, 1993.

- *Picking Apples and Pumpkins* by Amy Hutchings. Scholastic, 1994.

- *The Pumpkin Book* by Gail Gibbons. Holiday House, 2000.

- *Pumpkins* by Jacqueline Farmer. Charlesbridge, 2004.

- *The Seasons of Arnold's Apple Tree* by Gail Gibbons. Voyager Books, 1988.

Atlas Research

Major Pumpkin-Producing States

State	Capital City	Latitude	Longitude
Colorado			
California			
Ohio			
Georgia			
Maryland			
New Jersey			
Oregon			
Pennsylvania			
Rhode Island			
Washington			

Major Apple-Producing States

State	Capital City	Latitude	Longitude
Michigan			
California			
New York			
Virginia			
Pennsylvania			
Washington			

Pumpkins: True or False?

Directions: Use the encyclopedia to determine if the following statements are true or false. Record the page number where you located the fact that proved or disproved each statement.

		T/F	Page No.
1.	Pumpkins are related to cucumbers, melons and squash.	_____	_____
2.	Pumpkin flowers are edible.	_____	_____
3.	Pumpkins are large members of the berry family.	_____	_____
4.	In early colonial times, pumpkins were used as an ingredient for the crust of pies, not the filling.	_____	_____
5.	Pumpkins were once recommended for removing freckles and curing snakebites.	_____	_____
6.	Pumpkins will make you sick if you eat them raw.	_____	_____
7.	Pumpkins are fruit.	_____	_____
8.	Pumpkins ripen all year-round in the United States.	_____	_____
9.	Native Americans used pumpkin seeds for food and medicine.	_____	_____
10.	Pumpkins used to be considered poisonous.	_____	_____

Match These Apples

Directions: Examine the real apples in front of you. Each one has a number. Identify the apples using the terms below. Use each term only once.

Name: _____

Red Delicious; Granny Smith; Cortland; Fuji; Golden Delicious

1 _____

2 _____

3 _____

4 _____

5 _____

Owls, Bats, and Spiders

• Library Lessons •

by | Debra LaPlante

Spooky Research without Scary Results

With concerns in recent years about Halloween celebrations at school, my second grade team and I turned student interest and excitement about this season into a collaborative research project. The teachers' goals were for the students to find facts and write a report. Their spelling lists during this month included stories about owls, bats, and spiders. My goals were to make sure students understood using a table of contents and index to find facts, writing a bibliography to cite sources, and taking notes without copying. Though it was very early in the school year, we decided that by simplifying these processes, we could meet our goals and several of our standards at the same time. (*Note: If you can't get a whole team to work on this, begin with one interested teacher. "Scare up" a great research unit and watch collaboration grow!*)

Owls, bats, and spiders are natural choices for the month of October. They give students a chance to learn about some "scary" animals, dispel myths, and enjoy sharing the photos in nonfiction books with each other. You could add snakes, vultures, and other "scary" animals to the list of research topics. Some years we have a whole class do the same animal; sometimes we mix the three animals in the same class. The finished reports take the form of shape books that catch the whole school's attention when they are displayed on bulletin boards outside the classrooms.

A one-page Pie Research Form (see page 35) structures the research process into three chapters, with several facts per chapter. I begin using this pie form on large chart paper with my kindergartners so many of my students are familiar with it.

Preparation

Gather the nonfiction books you will need. Since we have a variety of reading levels, from students still at the first grade level to second graders reading at a fifth grade level, I pull a variety of books on each animal. Copy a Pie Research Form for each student and make a transparency of the sample visual on page 34. Have a few samples of completed shape books to show students what the finished product will look like. If you use a fixed schedule, plan with the teachers so you can work with each class for three days in a row. Teachers give up their time that cycle and get more time the next cycle so that everyone finishes during the month. This gives students a chance to research and write in one week rather than dragging the process out and needing to re-teach each session. Since my second grade team and I meet twice a cycle, this gives us enough time. We flex the schedule to accommodate this project.

Session 1: Excitement

At our school, teachers use literature rather than a spelling text to create spelling lists. Have the teacher read the owl, bat, or spider stories from which spelling words were chosen. When students come to the library, bring out the books, puppets, and a fun story to generate interest and excitement. I read a fiction story different from the story the teacher reads in the classroom. I also use puppets to have students brainstorm ideas about these animals. This gives me an idea of what the students know, and they get to share with each other. Have students look at the books. Some books have only one sentence per page for less-skilled readers. Teachers help guide students to books that match their level—a definite advantage of collaboration! Give students eight to ten minutes to examine the books. We discuss table of contents and index, and demonstrate looking for different topics to make sure students know how to find information using these tools. Set the chosen books aside, tagged with sticky notes showing students' names on each.

Session 2: Research Time

Before we begin, we brainstorm possible research topics on a whiteboard. The topics often include some that are too specific such as "How big is it?" and "How fast can it fly?" We write most suggestions on the board, then show students how to combine these into larger subjects. We erase topics that are too narrow and leave topics such as: appearance (size, color, shape, details), behavior (life cycle, predator, and prey), habitat (place, nests, homes), special traits and abilities for survival (poison, talons, camouflage), or diet. Students use the list to choose three questions to research which will form their chapters. We teach them to list large topics on the outside of the circle and note the facts on the inside.

I model this note-taking method using a book about a different animal. Students use a sample book and worksheet about echidnas to help me fill in the research form visual on the overhead. Since this is an unusual animal that most students are not familiar with, everyone is engaged and eager to find the facts and "help Mrs. LaPlante."

A simple bibliography—Before students begin using the Pie Research Form, have them find the title, author, and copyright date to write at the top of the form. This teaches students to give appropriate credit, and guarantees that they will get the same book they were using when they return to the library for future research.

Session 3: More Research

This is the final note-taking session. I teach students to read the information, then close the book to write down a phrase or record a fact for the topic on their Pie Research Forms. Because they can't see the author's words, they must remember what was important and record it in their own words. During this session, the teacher helps students who have missed sessions catch up while I check to see that students have enough facts in each category. If students have time, they can check another source such as the *World Book Student Discovery Encyclopedia* for more details to add. If they use an additional source, make sure they add it to the bibliography.

Session 4: It's Publishing Time

I begin by showing students samples of finished shape books again and giving instructions for completing the title page (title of the report, author, and the copyright date). Hand out a complete set of book forms in the appropriate shape to each student. They will transfer their bibliography information to the bibliography page in their shape book. After they finish all of the chapters, they will create a table of contents.

Give students file folders to store their papers (I reuse them each year), then have them use their Pie Research Forms to begin writing their "chapters." The number of pages will depend on their writing abilities and the size of their printing so leave numbering for the end. The goal for each chapter is to have three to four sentences on that chapter's question or topic. Help English language learners and special needs students express their ideas in writing as needed to complete this task. If necessary, continue this session in the classroom.

Session 5: Assembly and Presentations

The last collaborative session is devoted to students organizing their final pages to produce the book. The teachers, my assistant, and I make sure the book is in the proper order and insert the table of contents page and front and back covers. Once the books are stapled, the students number the pages and create the table of contents. When at least five students are finished, the teacher or I take that group to the story area to begin the presentations. It's amazing how quickly and neatly the remaining students work to be able to join the rest of the class. Teachers finish the presentations in the classroom if library time runs out.

This is an exciting month of research for the students. This year we added a bonus—a small wireless microphone/PA system that allowed even the quietest students to have a big voice and be a star performer.

Tips for Success:

- Keep the selected animals chosen to a small number and purchase enough books for each student to have a copy with a few extra to accommodate a range of abilities.

- Have students write to your state fish and game department to get more information about the animals as well as practice letter writing.

- Remember to pull the books from the library shelves **before** you or the teachers announce the project.

- If you use a fixed schedule, work with the team to juggle the schedule for more concentrated time for each teacher. Let teamwork and cooperation rule the day.

- Celebrate success. We always have a WOW (Wonders of Writing) night in April to show parents student writing from the whole year. You might add an evening Author Night for parents. Students will read their books to their parents. A drawing for free books will be sure to draw a crowd.

- Use this research to continue other writing lessons such as writing poetry.

Poetry Extension

We asked students to use a simple framework of adjectives to write cumulative poems about their animals. Here are a couple examples:

Owl
White owl
Hooting white owl
Sharp-clawed, hooting white owl
Big, sharp-clawed, hooting
white owl.

Bat
Furry bat
Small, furry bat
Swooping, small, furry bat
Shrieking, swooping, small,
furry bat.

See pages 36–47 for owl, bat, and spider shape book templates.

Pie Research Form Sample Visual

Title: _____

Author: _____

Copyright Date: _____

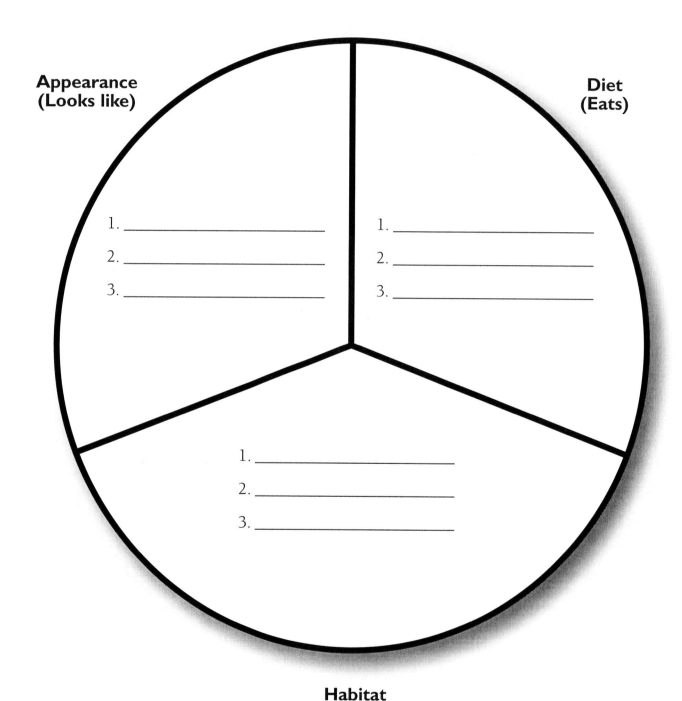

**Appearance
(Looks like)**

1. _____
2. _____
3. _____

**Diet
(Eats)**

1. _____
2. _____
3. _____

1. _____
2. _____
3. _____

**Habitat
(Lives)**

Pie Research Form

Title: _____

Author: _____

Copyright Date: _____

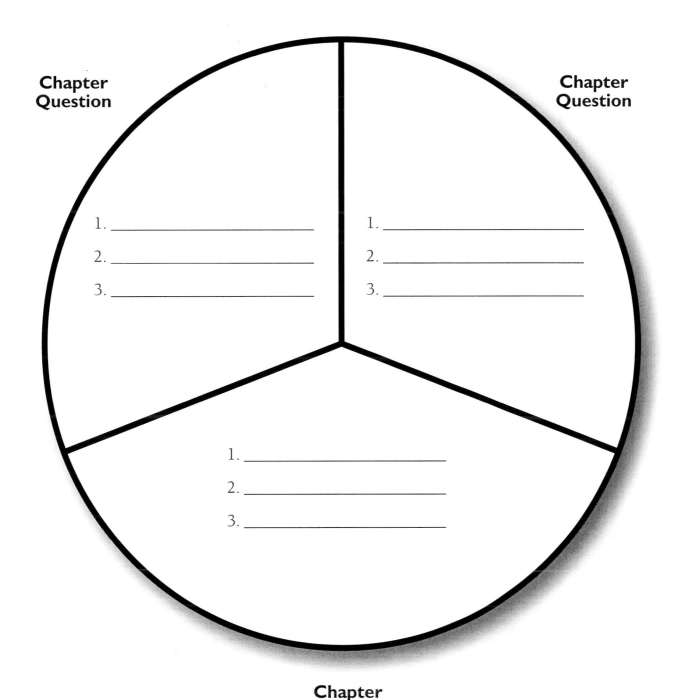

Chapter Question

1. _____
2. _____
3. _____

Chapter Question

1. _____
2. _____
3. _____

Chapter Question

1. _____
2. _____
3. _____

Title: _____

Author: _____

Copyright Date: _____

Table of Contents

_____ p. _____

_____ p. _____

_____ p. _____

Bibliography

_____

Author's Name: last, first

_____

Title

_____

Copyright Date

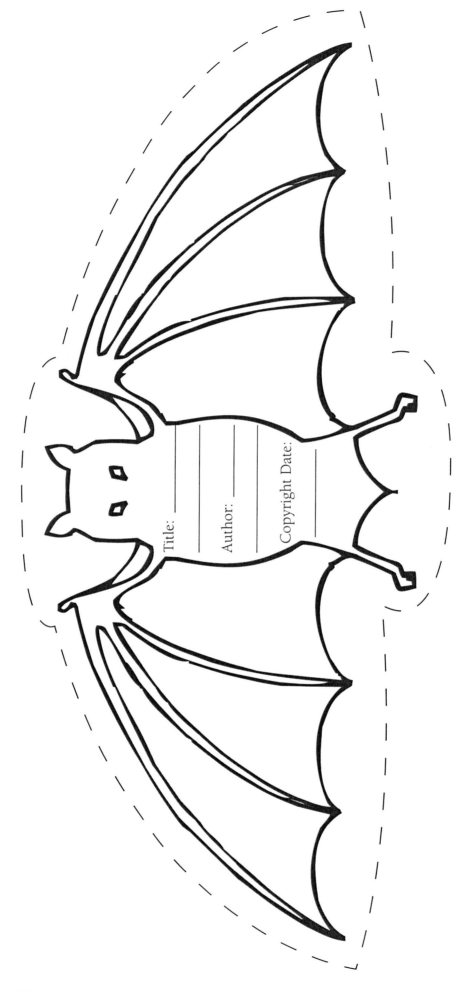

Title: _____

Author: _____

Copyright Date: _____

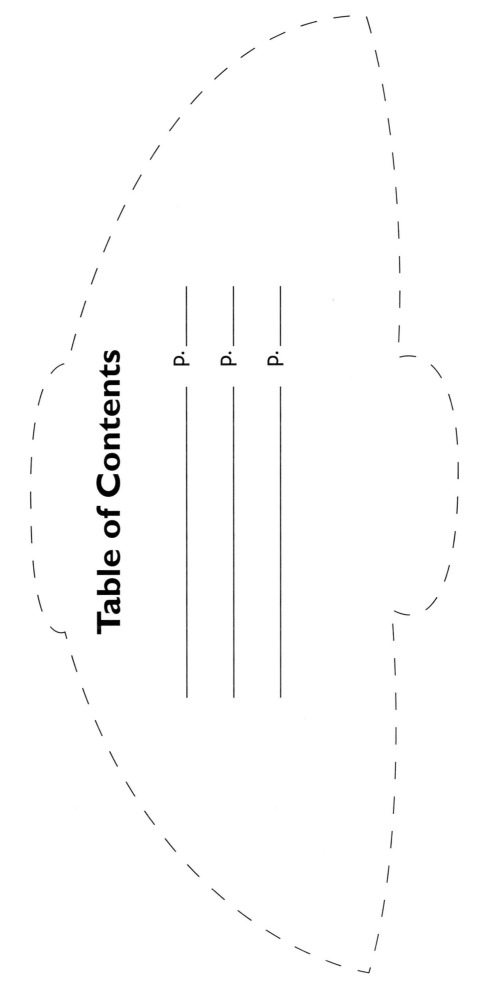

Table of Contents

p. _____

p. _____

p. _____

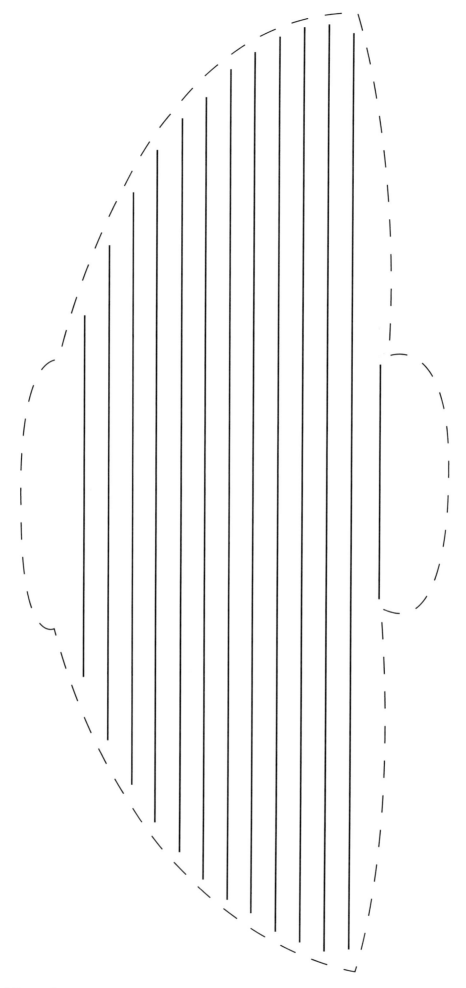

Bibliography

Author's Name: last, first

Title

Copyright Date

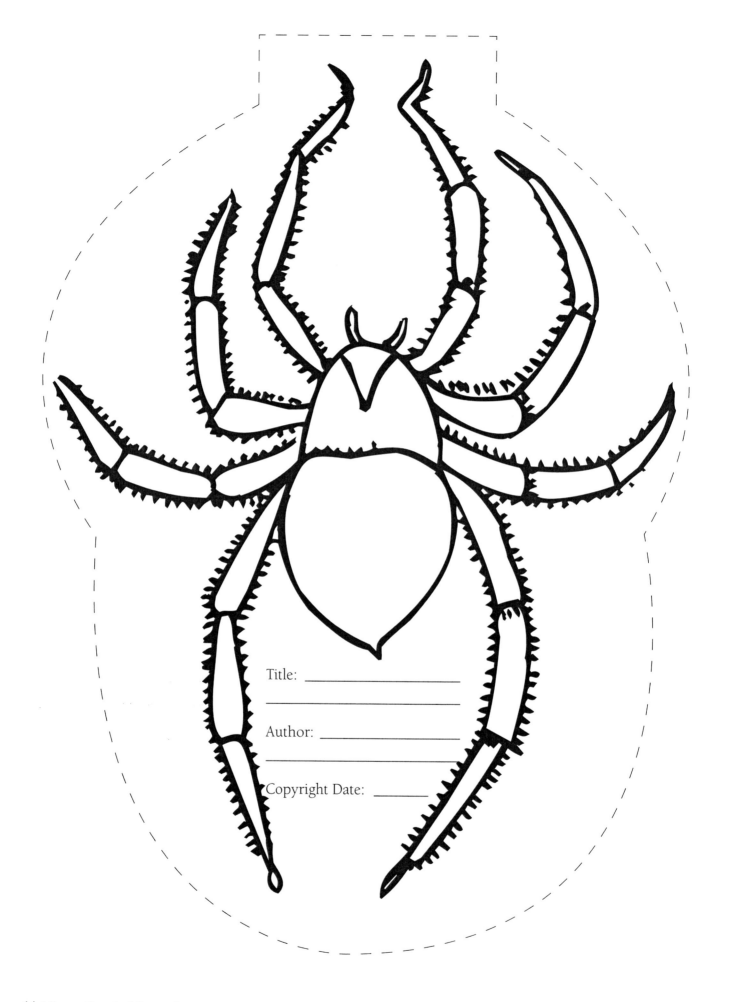

Title: _____

_____

Author: _____

_____

Copyright Date: _____

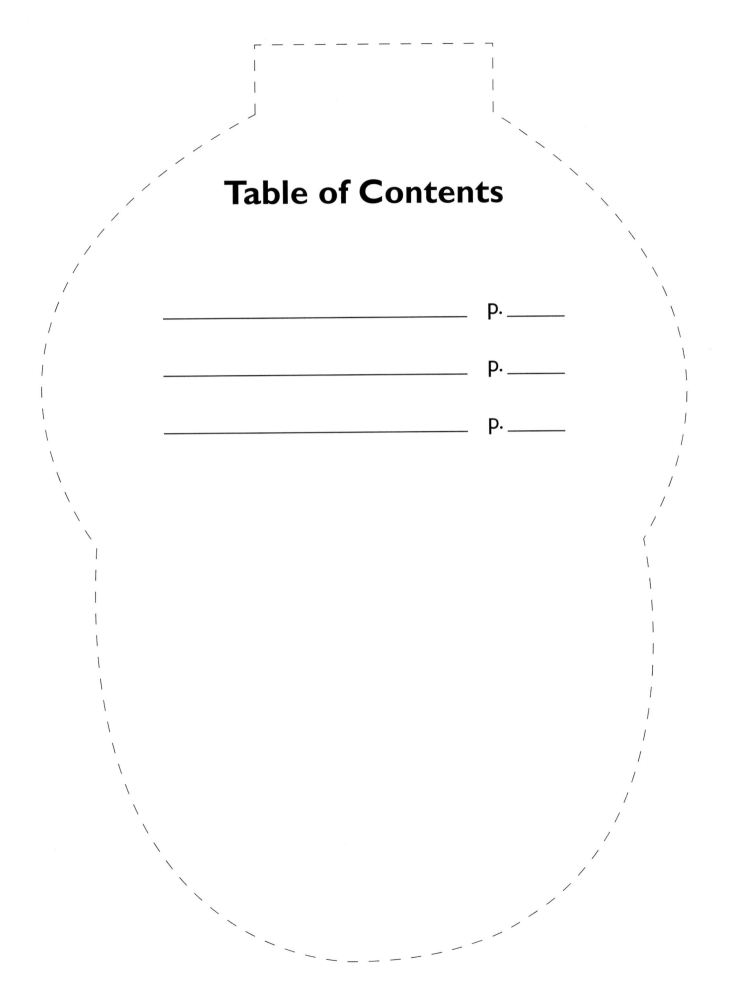

Table of Contents

_____ p. _____

_____ p. _____

_____ p. _____

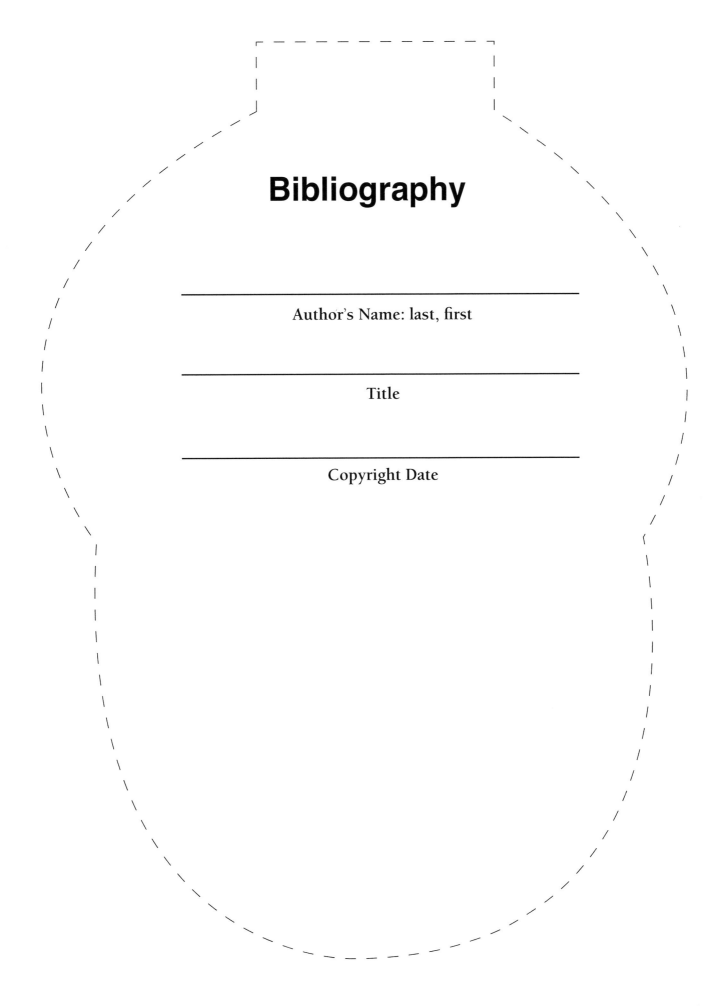

Bibliography

_____

Author's Name: last, first

_____

Title

_____

Copyright Date

The Marauder's Map

• Library Lessons •

by | Lynne Farrell Stover

Grades 3–5

J.K. Rowling is adept at stressing the importance of educational tools and the role they play in the lives of young wizards at Hogwarts School for Witchcraft and Wizardry. Books, newspapers, maps, and time-turners all assume a significant role in advancing the plot and saving the day. It is during Harry Potter's third year at Hogwarts that twins Fred and George Weasley give our hero an early Christmas present, the Marauder's Map. This magical piece of parchment not only depicts all of the logistical aspects of Hogwarts but also reveals the current location of every person on the school's grounds.

In our Muggle schools, mapping skills are taught at every grade level. Often students and teachers need to be reminded that the library is a treasure house of maps of all kinds. Use Harry Potter's Marauder's Map as a hook to encourage students to use the media center's many resources while participating in geography, history, and literature review activities.

 ## Lesson I: Puzzling Map Key

Description
A "key" to having a good education is not necessarily knowing everything but rather knowing where to find the specific information needed. As Harry Potter must often do to uncover information, students will assemble a puzzle to help them discover the vocabulary of mapping terms.

Objective
Students will review definitions of different types of maps and reference books that contain maps, graphs, and charts.

Materials
* Puzzling Map Key boards and pieces (see pages 51–52)

* envelopes

* scissors

* examples of various maps, atlases, almanacs, and globes

Procedure
1. Prepare the boards and puzzle pieces prior to class. Each student or group will need a board and an envelope containing pre-cut puzzle pieces. Note: Photocopying the pieces on different colors of paper allows for easier construction of the puzzle and makes it easier to keep the pieces separated into individual envelopes.

2. Introduce the activity by explaining that maps are informative tools that have existed for as long as man has traveled from one place to another. Ask students to suggest some uses for maps. (Possible answers: To travel to unknown places, to document what land you own, to know where your enemy is in wartime, to mark where a buried treasure is located.)

3. Show students examples of the maps, globes, atlases, and almanacs available in your library.

4. Pass out the boards and envelopes containing the puzzle pieces.

5. Have students construct their puzzles on the board. The term on the puzzle piece corresponds to a definition on the board. Explain that this "hands on" activity is a method some people find very effective in studying for quizzes and tests.

6. Give students a few minutes to study before the quiz below.

7. Have students turn their boards over. Instruct them to hold up the correct puzzle piece for each definition you read. Conduct the quiz. Scan the room for students' answers after each question.

8. Ask students how well they did on the quiz. Was working with the puzzle the "key" to their success?

9. Have students place the puzzle pieces back in the envelopes.

Puzzling Map Quiz

1. What type of map shows the height of land above sea level? **Relief Map**

2. What do we call a model of the earth? **Globe**

3. What type of map shows how many people live in a specific place? **Population Density Map**

4. A map that shows national and state boundaries is what kind of map? **Political Map**

5. What is a book of maps called? **Atlas**

6. What kind of map would you use to travel in your car to the next state? **Road Map**

7. What kind of book contains many types of information, including maps, charts, and tables? **Almanac**

8. What kind of map shows the earth's natural features? **Physical Map**

Lesson 2: Marauder's Map Projects

Description: The settings in *Harry Potter and the Prisoner of Azkaban*, as in all of J. K. Rowling's works, are truly remarkable. Readers can easily visualize the busy shops on Diagon Alley and the streets teeming with students in Hogsmeade on special visiting days. Drawing maps of these imaginary places can be fun for students. They enjoy the freedom of depicting a place that does not really exist. Moreover, specific mapping fundamentals must be understood and reflected in the finished project.

Objective

The student will create a map of an imaginary place. This map will include a title, compass rose, key, and scale.

Materials

- copies of the Marauder's Map worksheet (see master on page 53)
- paper, pencils, colored pencils, rulers
- atlases and road maps for student reference (optional)

Procedures

1. Prepare copies of the worksheet. Allow students to work individually or in groups. Gather materials for students to use in creating their maps.

2. Tell students that they will draw a map of an imaginary place. Ask if they know any imaginary settings from books they have read. (Possible answers: Narnia, Neverland, Oz, Middle-earth)

3. Pass out worksheets and mapping materials.

4. Go over the directions and project choices.

5. Allow students about twenty minutes to complete the project. Note: Some students may wish to add more detail and require more time. Allow them to complete their maps at home.

6. Have students share their completed maps with the class. Maps may also be displayed on a bulletin board or placed in a three-ring binder to create a class atlas of imaginary places.

Lesson 3: Maps Are Magic Jeopardy

Description
Because Harry Potter is able to read the magical Marauder's Map, he is at a distinct advantage while taking the risk of visiting the village of Hogsmeade. Knowing specific facts and taking risks will also put students at an advantage when playing the Maps are Magic Jeopardy game.

Objectives
- Students will use knowledge of maps, literature and history to participate in a class activity.

- Students will use game strategy and math skills while participating in a class activity.

Materials
- Maps Are Magic Jeopardy answer game board (see page 54)

- Maps Are Magic Jeopardy questions key (see page 55)

- paper and pencil for each team to keep score

- pencils or pens

Procedure
1. Prior to the lesson, create a method for using game cards. You can make a transparency of the questions and use sticky notes to cover the answers until a category is selected. Or make a game board by creating twenty-five construction paper or book pockets to hold the answer cards. (To facilitate easy replacement of game cards, either write the category on the back of each card or run off each category on a different color of paper.)

2. Divide the class into three groups. Each group will need a scorekeeper and a spokesperson. The spokesperson is responsible for conferring with team members to choose game card and for stating the question that corresponds with the answer on the card. The scorekeeper keeps a tally of points earned by all three teams. Scores will be compared at the end of the game. The team with the highest points wins. Note: This lesson is intended as an introduction or review, so give credit for "close enough" answers.

3. The group with the oldest member may be Team A. The group with the youngest member Team B and the remaining group Team C.

4. Start with Team A. Read the answer for the chosen category. If the team does not state the correct question, another team may volunteer to state the question and earn the points. However, Team B will be the next to choose from the game board so that all teams have equal opportunity to score. No points will be deducted for incorrect responses.

5. Play until time runs out and all game cards have been used.

Puzzling Map Key Board

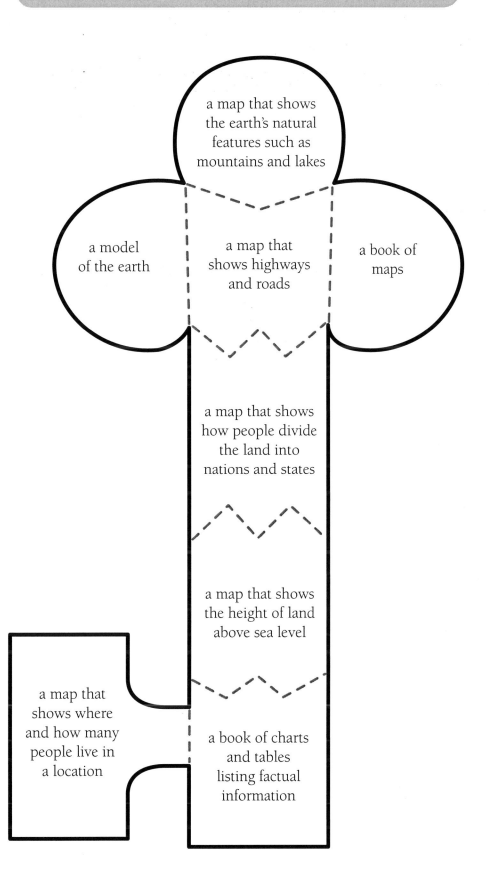

a map that shows the earth's natural features such as mountains and lakes

a model of the earth

a map that shows highways and roads

a book of maps

a map that shows how people divide the land into nations and states

a map that shows the height of land above sea level

a map that shows where and how many people live in a location

a book of charts and tables listing factual information

Puzzling Map Key Pieces

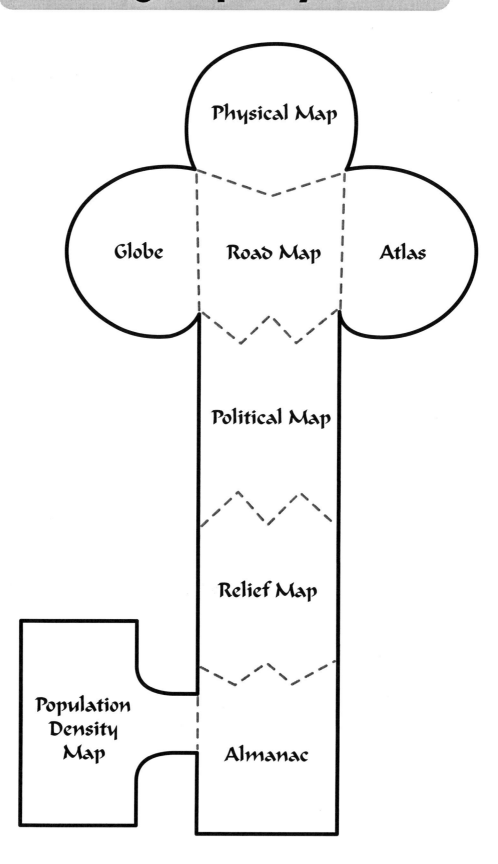

Physical Map

Globe | Road Map | Atlas

Political Map

Relief Map

Population Density Map

Almanac

Marauder's Map

Read over the possible mapping projects below. Choose one you would like to do. Using the materials provided, create an attractive map.

Each map should include:

- **Title**—tells you the map's subject and the physical area it represents.
- **Compass Rose**—identifies north, south, east and west.
- **Scale**—helps relate distances on the map to the actual area represented.
- **Key**—explains identifying lines, symbols, colors, and shading used.
- **Labels**—identify points of interest.

Possible projects:

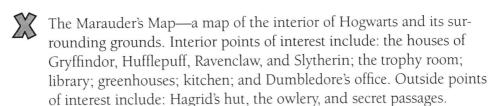 The Marauder's Map—a map of the interior of Hogwarts and its surrounding grounds. Interior points of interest include: the houses of Gryffindor, Hufflepuff, Ravenclaw, and Slytherin; the trophy room; library; greenhouses; kitchen; and Dumbledore's office. Outside points of interest include: Hagrid's hut, the owlery, and secret passages.

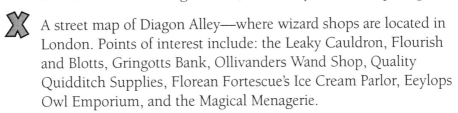 A street map of Diagon Alley—where wizard shops are located in London. Points of interest include: the Leaky Cauldron, Flourish and Blotts, Gringotts Bank, Ollivanders Wand Shop, Quality Quidditch Supplies, Florean Fortescue's Ice Cream Parlor, Eeylops Owl Emporium, and the Magical Menagerie.

A town map of Hogsmeade—the wizard village near Hogwarts. Points of interest include the Shrieking Shack, Zonko's Joke Shop, Dervish and Banges, Hog's Head Pub, Three Broomsticks, Honeydukes, and the Hogsmeade Post Office.

A map of your choice.

Maps Are Magic Jeopardy

Answers

Types of Maps	Literary Places	Explorers	Potter's Places	Mapping Terms
10 Roap Map	**10** Munchkin Land	**10** He sailed the ocean blue in 1492	**10** Harry's School	**10** Compass Rose
20 Physical Map	**20** Narnia	**20** The place that John Smith settled.	**20** A street of stores where wizards shops.	**20** Equator
30 Political Map	**30** Neverland	**30** Norse explorer– the son of Eric the Red.	**30** An all-wizard village near Harry's school.	**30** Scale Bar
40 Population Density Map	**40** Middle-earth	**40** He explored the Hudson River	**40** The dark woods surrounding Harry's School	**40** Key
50 Relief Map	**50** Lilliput	**50** He reached the North Pole in 1909.	**50** Where students board the Hogwarts Express.	**50** Axis

Maps Are Magic Jeopardy

Questions

Types of Maps	Literary Places	Explorers	Potter's Places	Mapping Terms
10 What map shows highways and roads?	**10** What is the name of the first place Dorothy lands in *The Wizard of Oz* stories?	**10** Who is Christopher Columbus?	**10** What is Hogwarts?	**10** What symbol on a map shows direction?
20 What map shows the earth's natural features?	**20** What is the name of the place in *The Lion, the Witch and the Wardrobe?* (Or other stories by C.S. Lewis)	**20** What is Jamestown?	**20** What is Diagon Alley?	**20** What is the imaginary line around the middle of the earth?
30 What map shows how humans have divided the land?	**30** Where does Peter Pan live in the *Peter Pan* stories?	**30** Who is Leif Ericsson?	**30** What is Hogsmeade?	**30** What is the symbol used on a map to show distance?
40 What map shows a location and how many people live there?	**40** What is the name of the place in *The Lord of the Rings* trilogy?	**40** Who is Henry Hudson?	**40** What is the Forbidden Forest?	**40** What part of a map informs you about the meaning of the symbols?
50 What map shows the height of the terrain above sea level?	**50** What is the name of a place in *Gulliver's Travels?*	**50** Who is Robert Peary?	**50** What is Platform Nine and Three-Quarters?	**50** What is the imaginary line that runs through the center of the earth from the North Pole to the South Pole?

Inkheart: Parts of a Book and More

• Library Lessons •

by | Lynn Farrell Stover

Grades 3–6

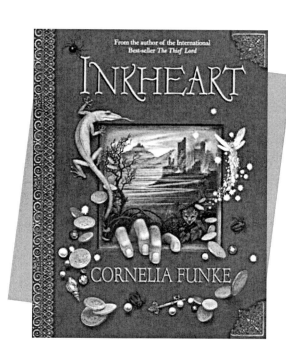

As with her acclaimed book *The Thief Lord*, popular German author Cornelia Funke's book *Inkheart* has many young fans. A story within a story, this fantasy novel celebrates the book. From Mo, twelve-year-old Meggie's bookbinder father, to Great-Aunt Elinor, an avid book collector who likes books more than she likes most people, the characters are compelling and well written. Readers of this tale are treated to information about the history of book-making, the care of books, and book collectors and collections.

The following lessons and activities are appropriate for grades 3–6, but may be adapted for older students. Each lesson stands alone and begins with a quote from *Inkheart*. The quotes were added to provide a connection between the lesson and the story. They may be shared aloud to set the tone, but have not been incorporated in the lesson itself. Students need not be familiar with the book to complete the lessons.

Lesson I: Parts of a Book Round Table

"Every book should begin with attractive endpapers. Preferably in a dark color: dark red or dark blue, depending on the binding. When you open the book it's like going to the theater. First you see the curtain. Then it's pulled aside and the show begins."
—Meggie's father, Mortimer Folchart, a bookbinder

Time Required: 20–30 minutes

Objectives

- Review the parts of a book.
- Participate in a prepared question and answer activity using concepts from *Inkheart* to explore parts of a book.

Materials

- Parts of a Book Roundtable Q&A Cards, ideally copied on colored paper, glued to 3" x 5" index cards, and laminated for reuse (see pages 59–60)
- Parts of a Book Roundtable Answer Grid for teacher use (see page 61)
- optional: a copy of *Inkheart* to display

Procedure

1. Prepare Parts of a Book Roundtable cards before class. Each card should have a question on the front and the answer to a different question on the back. For example, the first card should read "**(First Question Asked) Question**: Mortimer Folchart, also known as Mo, repairs old and damaged books. What is a good title for Mo's job?" on one side. The back should read, "**Answer**: The **index**, in the back of a book, lists the book's topics and page numbers."

2. Introduce the activity based on *Inkheart* by Cornelia Funke. Assure students that they do not need to have read the book, but they do need to listen carefully because this lesson focuses on the definitions for parts of a book.

3. Distribute prepared Q&A cards to students. There are twelve cards, so either have students work in pairs or explain that not everyone will have a card.

4. Prompt the student with the card labeled "First Question Asked" to read his question to the class. Have students study the answer side of their cards to see if they have the answer to that question. The student with the appropriate card ("There are several good titles for what Mo does for a living. He could be called a book restorer, book binder, or book doctor") replies by reading the answer. That student then turns the card over and asks the question, "One of the first things Mo does to help a book look better is to give it a new outside. What is another name for a book's outside?" This continues until the student who asked the first question answers the last one. Show examples of each book part as its question is asked and answered.

5. Review the activity by holding up a book and asking the students to name its parts as you point to them.

Lesson 2: Books Through the Ages

"Once only the rich people could read, so the pictures painted around the letters were to help the poor to understand the stories, too. . . . The books were put in churches, and a page was turned every day to show a new picture."
–Great-Aunt Elinor explaining illumination

Time Required: 20–25 minutes

Objective
• Participate in a class activity about the history books.

Materials
• Books through the Ages visual/worksheet on page 62
• overhead projector and water-soluble marker
• optional: a copy of *Inkheart* to display

Procedure
1. Explain that the students will learn about the historical development of books. You may need to explain the concepts of BC and AD.
2. Show the visual, read the directions and solicit answers from students. Note: Alternatively, this transparency may be used as an individual or group worksheet.
3. Record student responses. Answers: 1. clay; 2. papyrus; 3. wax; 4. scrolls; 5. paper; 6. illuminated; 7. type; 8. Gutenberg; 9. dime novel; 10. computer.
4. If time allows, discuss ideas about the future of the book. Start with this question: "Do you think computers will ever completely replace books? Why or why not?"

Lesson 3: Fantastic Heroines & Vile Villains

"'Indeed, he wanted revenge,' Meggie read on. If only her voice weren't shaking so much, but it wasn't easy to kill, even if someone else was going to do it for her. 'So the Shadow went to his master and reached out to him with ashen hands . . .'"
–*Inkheart*

Time Required: 15–20 minutes

Objective

- Student will demonstrate knowledge of literary characters.

Materials

- Fantastic Heroines & Vile Villains activity sheet (see page 63)
- writing tools
- optional: copies of featured books for students to check out

Procedure

1. Prepare and collect materials prior to class.

2. Introduce the lesson by telling the students that today's activity will feature children's books that have girls as main characters.

3. Distribute activity sheets. Read the introduction and directions aloud. Students may work individually or in groups. Note: All of the featured heroines and villains have appeared in popular movies and should be familiar to many students.

4. Check for understanding:

   1-H Wendy Darling & Captain Hook (*Peter Pan* by J. M. Barrie)

   2-D Violet Baudelaire & Count Olaf (A Series of Unfortunate Events by Lemony Snicket)

   3-B Lucy Pevensie & The White Witch (*The Lion, the Witch and the Wardrobe* by C. S. Lewis)

   4-J Alice & The Queen of Hearts (*Alice's Adventures in Wonderland* by Lewis Carroll)

   5-G Meg Murry & IT (*A Wrinkle in Time* by Madeline L'Engle)

   6- E Lyra Belacqua & Mrs. Coulter (*The Golden Compass* by Philip Pullman)

   7-C Matilda Wormwood & Headmistress Agatha Trunchbull (*Matilda* by Roald Dahl)

   8- I Mallory Grace & Mulgarath (The Spiderwick Chronicles by Toni DiTerlizzi and Holly Black)

   9-A Hermione Granger & Lord Voldemort (the Harry Potter series by J. K. Rowling)

   10-F Dorothy Gale & The Wicked Witch of the West (*The Wonderful Wizard of Oz* by L. Frank Baum)

Parts of a Book Roundtable Q&A Cards

Copy the cards below on colored paper. Then cut along the dotted lines and glue each question and the answer next to it on a 3" x 5" index card. Laminate for reuse.

First Question Asked

Question: Mortimer Folchart, also known as Mo, repairs old and damaged books. What is a good title for Mo's job?

Answer: The **index**, in the back of a book, lists the book's topics and page numbers.

Question: One of the first things Mo does to help a book look better is to give it a new outside. What is another name for a book's outside?

Answer: There are many possible titles for Mo's job. He could be called a book restorer, book binder, or "book doctor."

Question: Mo's daughter, Meggie, loves to read. She knows there are other names for the **introduction** to a book. What are they?

Answer: A book's outside is called a cover. (Mo knows you shouldn't "judge a book by its cover," but he likes his restored books to look good.)

Question: A book's **dedication** is a message from the author thanking someone for his or her help. What might be a good dedication for a book titled *The Best Books in the World*?

Answer: A book's **introduction** explains what the book is about. An introduction can also be called a **forward**, **prologue**, or **preface**.

Question: Where would Meggie look to find out how many chapters are in a book?

Answer: The **dedication** for a book entitled The Best Books in the World could be, "To Mrs. Reed, the librarian who helped me find all the great books."

Question: Why does Mo write the title of a book on its **spine**?

Answer: Meggie would look at the **table of contents** to find out how many chapters are in the book.

Parts of a Book Roundtable Q&A Cards

Question: What is the story or text of a book called?

Answer: Mo writes the title of the book on its spine because it's the part of the book that shows when it's on the shelf.

Question: Where would Mo look to find out the year a book was published?

Answer: The story or text of a book is called the **body** of the book. It's the biggest part of a book.

Question: One of Meggie's favorite science books has an excellent glossary. What is a **glossary**?

Answer: To find out the year a book was published, Mo would look in the front of the book on the **copyright page**.

Question: Meggie discovered her favorite book also contained a bibliography. Why did this discovery make Meggie happy?

Answer: A **glossary** is a list of special words found in the book and their definitions.

Question: Mo is repairing a rare book that contains a detailed appendix. What is an **appendix**?

Answer: Maggie was happy because a **bibliography** is a list of books that relate to the subject of the book. Now she knows about some other books she would like to read.

Question: What part of Meggie's favorite book would list all the topics discussed in the book as well as the pages where the information could be found?

Answer: An **appendix** is located in the back of a book and contains extra information such as charts, lists, and tables.

Parts of a Book Roundtable Answer Grid

First Question Asked	
Question: Mortimer Folchart, also known as Mo, repairs old and damaged books. What is a good title for Mo's job?	**Answer**: There are many possible titles for Mo's job. He could be called a book restorer, book binder, or "book doctor."
Question: One of the first things Mo does to help a book look better is to give it a new outside. What is another name for a book's outside?	**Answer**: A book's outside is called a cover. (Mo knows you shouldn't "judge a book by its cover," but he likes his restored books to look good.)
Question: Mo's daughter, Meggie, loves to read. She knows there are other names for the introduction to a book. What are they?	**Answer**: A book's introduction explains what the book is about. An introduction can also be called a forward, prologue, or preface.
Question: A book's dedication is a message from the author thanking someone for his or her help. What might be a good dedication for a book entitled The Best Books in the World?	**Answer**: The dedication for a book entitled The Best Books in the World could be, "To Mrs. Reed, the librarian who helped me find all the great books."
Question: Where would Meggie look to find out how many chapters are in a book?	**Answer**: Meggie would look at the table of contents to find out how many chapters are in the book.
Question: Why does Mo write the title of a book on its spine?	**Answer**: Mo writes the title of the book on its spine because it's the part of the book that shows when it's on the shelf.
Question: What is the story or text of a book called?	**Answer**: The story or text of a book is called the body of the book. It's the biggest part of a book.
Question: Where would Mo look to find out the year a book was published?	**Answer**: To find out the year a book was published, Mo would look in the front of the book on the copyright page.
Question: One of Meggie's favorite science books has an excellent glossary. What is a glossary?	**Answer**: A glossary is a list of special words found in the book and their definitions.
Question: Meggie discovered her favorite book also contained a bibliography. Why did this discovery make Meggie happy?	**Answer**: Maggie was happy because a bibliography is a list of books that relate to the subject of the book. Now she knows about some other books she would like to read.
Question: Mo is repairing a rare book that contains a detailed appendix. What is an appendix?	**Answer**: An appendix is located in the back of a book and contains extra information such as charts, lists, and tables.
Question: What part of Meggie's favorite book would list all the topics discussed in the book as well as the pages where the information could be found?	**Answer**: The index, in the back of a book, lists the book's topics and page numbers.

Books Through the Ages

Learn a quick history of the book by using the words in the scroll below to complete the rhymes.

3500 BC

Way back in the Sumerian's day,
writing was done on tablets of _____.

2400 BC

For Egyptians, writing was no big fuss.
They wrote hieroglyphics on _____.

500 BC

The Greeks wrote notes and figured their tax
on wooden tablets they covered with _____.

295 BC

King Ptolemy's library had ambitious goals.
Some say said it contained 500,000 _____.

150 BC

In China a wonderful thing did occur! The people
created the first useful _____.

500 AD

Middle Ages manuscripts were highly decorated.
Scribes created pages that were _____.

1300 AD

In Korea, without much fanfare or hype,
inventors produced the first moveable _____.

1450 AD

In this year in Germany, in case you haven't heard,
the printing press was invented by Johann _____.

1885 AD

Many books could now be printed—there were
lots and lots to sell! One kind that readers really
liked was called the _____ _____.

The Future

Will any of our printed books still be there on the
scene, or will all our stories and our news be on a
computer _____?

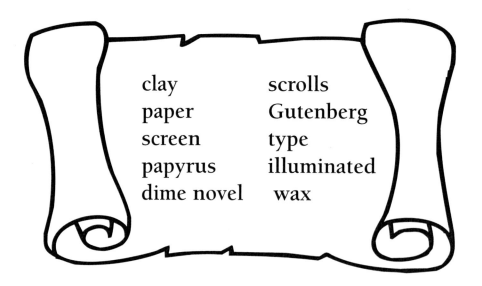

clay   scrolls
paper   Gutenberg
screen   type
papyrus   illuminated
dime novel   wax

Fantastic Heroines & Vile Villains

Meggie Folchart is brave, strong, and resourceful. She is the heroine in *Inkheart* by Cornelia Funke. Another character in the same book is Capricorn who is cruel, horrible, and selfish. He is the villain.

Directions: Match the literary heroines on the left to their corresponding villains on the right.

___ 1. Wendy Darling	A. Lord Voldemort
___ 2. Violet Baudelaire	B. The White Witch
___ 3. Lucy Pevensie	C. Headmistress Agatha Trunchbull
___ 4. Alice	D. Count Olaf
___ 5. Meg Murry	E. Mrs. Coulter
___ 6. Lyra Belacqua	F. The Wicked Witch of the West
___ 7. Matilda Wormwood	G. IT
___ 8. Mallory Grace (sister of Jared & Simon)	H. Captain Hook
	I. Mulgarath
___ 9. Hermione Granger	J. The Queen of Hearts
___ 10. Dorothy Gale	

The Mind Is a Wonderful Thing to Use

• Library Lessons •

by | Pat Miller

Metacognition

I went to an interesting workshop recently about helping students as young as five to think about their own thinking, with suggestions for helping them develop thinking skills such as visualizing, connecting, etc. The workshop was given by Dr. Jean Lowery, LMS, in the New Haven Public Schools at the Tennessee Association of School Librarians Annual Conference. This article is based on the thinking I did about the thinking she presented to us—otherwise called "metacognition."

The human brain is not only busy, it is demanding. Though it only weighs three pounds, it consumes twenty percent of a person's oxygen intake each day. A fifth of the blood pumped by the heart goes to the brain. The brain sends tiny electrical signals to all parts of the body at speeds reaching 200 miles per hour. The gray matter in our head is more complicated and capable than a supercomputer, allowing us to think about the mundane and the divine, and even to think about *itself*. That is what metacognition is, and it can be developed beginning in pre-kindergarten.

The six skills of metacognition mentioned by Dr. Lowery are:

- noticing
- wondering
- picturing
- connecting
- predicting
- figuring out

What Do I Notice about the Story?

You activate a child's ability to notice when you point out the parts of a book. When your hand sweeps across the page in the direction that you are reading, you encourage your youngest students to notice how reading progresses. Point out to them how the size of font can tell you how loudly to read the words, and that the punctuation tells you when to pause or raise your voice in a question or exclamation.

A key skill for pre-readers is to notice that the black marks on paper tell you what to say. Use books like *Yo, Yes?* by Chris Raschka and *No, David!* by David Shannon to help these children "read" a book with you after several repetitions. Wordless books are excellent for developing skills of noticing and of talking about what's going on in a story. (See page 68 for a bibliography of wordless books.)

You can also use some of the I Spy books by Jean Marzollo and Walter Wick. These popular books include simpler board books for the youngest students and encourage young minds to observe, compare, and discern. They are great brain books.

In *Alphabet City* by Stephen T. Johnson, students look at realistic paintings of things in an urban landscape to see letters of the alphabet. For example, a side view of a traffic signal forms the letter E, and fire escape steps make a Z along an apartment building wall. Students will have to examine some pictures very closely, especially when the letter is formed by negative space.

Books by Jan Brett are good for helping children notice picture clues because much of the story is told in the side bar illustrations. Children enjoy noticing the armadillo baby wandering into mischief in the side panels of *Armadillo Rodeo*, or observing which animal will next discover *The Mitten*.

Use poetry books to have children notice language like similes or onomatopoeia. Two very good ones to use with young children are *Here's a Little Poem: A Very First Book of Poetry* compiled by Jane Yolen and Andrew Fusek Peters, and *The Random House Book of Poetry for Children* compiled by Jack Prelutsky.

Read mysteries from age-appropriate series like Nate the Great (Marjorie Sharmat), Young Cam Jansen (David A. Adler), or The High Rise Private Eyes (Cynthia Rylant). These mysteries allow primary students to notice clues that will lead them to figure out the solution before the characters do.

When you share books, tell students to use their skills of noticing to help them think when they don't understand something. I recently was reading the biography of Sarah Hale by Laurie Halse Anderson. A repeated line proclaimed that she was "bold and brave and stubborn and smart." After the second time I read the line, a first grader asked why I kept saying she was bold when it looked like she had long brown hair. He was noticing and thinking, and something was amiss in his mind.

Noticing helps children tell whether the author has done something tricky. Recently I read *Adventures of Cow, Too* by Lori Korchek. By the third page something was very wrong. The words read, "Cow jumped for joy." The picture showed the squeezable cow toy standing next to a shopping list. The next page read, "Cow took a train to the store," but showed the cow perched like a hood ornament on the front of a school bus. What? This is where your students' powers of observation will kick in to make sense of this book. Once they "get it," they will love the humor of this naïve little cow who manages to succeed on his misguided adventure.

Children will also enjoy the antics of Minerva Louise (Janet Morgan Stoeke), a chicken who guesses wrong about things, but manages to make it all come out okay. For example, in *A Hat for Minerva Louise*, she mistakes a pair of mittens for two hats. They turn out to be perfect to keep both of her ends warm!

Noticing is also what helps children guess what an object is. This comes in handy with several books that involve scrutiny of the picture, a guess about the object or animal, and a page turn to reveal the correct answer. *The Look Book* by Tanya Hoban shows parts of items viewed through cutaways, inviting children to identify the object. Focusing our attention on a small part of a whole is great exercise for our noticing powers.

Around the Pond: Who's Been Here? by Lindsay Barrett George shows students tracks, bits of nests, etc., for students to guess which animal was there. Others in the series allow children to notice items on postcards from across the globe, in the woods, in the snow, and in the garden. It's fun for students to see if they have guessed right or wrong, and a lot of learning slips in along the way.

What Do I Wonder about the Story?

Before reading, especially nonfiction, ask students to examine the cover of the book and think about what they know about the topic. Then ask them, "What do you wonder?" They may think of questions based on the picture clues of the book's cover, or based on gaps in their schema (previous knowledge and concepts) about the topic. In the example given above about Sarah Hale, students wondered from the cover if she made the American flag (one was on the cover), if she was from "the olden days" (she was holding a quill pen), if she was a good writer, and why was the title *Thank You, Sarah*?

If you want to organize their questions, you can use the traditional K-W-L chart (what we Know, what we Want to know, what we Learned). I designed a chart I like better (see page 69) because it gives them space to wonder and space to revisit their wonderings to see what they learned.

The first column taps into their schema, the third their wondering. The second and fourth use the text to verify what they thought they knew and to answer the questions they developed before the reading.

Students may also wonder about what might happen next, why the author wrote this story, what's going on, and how it will end. They may wonder about the illustrative style. After I shared the Caldecott Medal-winner *My Friend Rabbit* by Eric Rohmann with a kindergarten class, one child blurted out in frustration, "But what does it MEAN?" At the book's end, he was still wondering what was going on.

Two good books to encourage wonder are *The Wolf's Chicken Stew* by Keiko Kasza (Will the wolf really eat the chicken when he discovers she has dozens of chicks?), and *Wolf's Coming!* by Joe Kulka. (Why are the animals hiding? It turns out they are having a surprise party for wolf!) You will hear audible wonder when you share the pop-up books of Robert Sabuda.

How Do I Picture the Story?

Picturing is what children do as they hear a story, especially if they cannot see the pictures. Alternate your read alouds with storytelling and tell the story without the text or illustrations. Afterward, have students discuss what they imagined seeing, hearing, touching, smelling, and tasting. I tell Gail E. Haley's *A Story, A Story*, the folktale about how Anansi fulfilled three difficult tasks to earn the stories of the sky god for all the people. The tasks involve catching Mmboro, the hornets that sting like fire, Mmotia, the fairy that men have never seen, and Osebo, the leopard with the terrible teeth. For each, Anansi devises a clever way to catch them.

The three catching scenes and the three tricky characters all make good subjects for students to illustrate. Amazingly, they can picture these even though they haven't seen them. I frequently point out the power of their imaginations. Recently we shared a story that involved gingerbread. At the end, I was going to give them each a ginger snap. I broke it in front of them and made a big deal of smelling the ginger and reacting to it. Then I asked, "Can you smell it?" They could—in their imaginations.

Another great book for picturing is *We're Going on a Bear Hunt* by Michael Rosen. Read or do it aloud without the pictures and ask children to come with you and picture themselves hunting for a B-I-G bear on a beautiful day. They should see and hear and smell the squishy mud, the cold blowy snow, and the dank, dark cave.

How Does This Connect to My Schema?

As students read or listen, they should be making connections to the schema in their heads. The most basic and familiar connection will be to themselves and their own lives: "This reminds me of when I ..." The next level would be to compare the story to things in the real world outside themselves: "This makes me think about ..." Finally, with your help in widening their literary repertoire, they will make connections to another book.

At first, ask and encourage students to explain the personal connections they make with books. When you've done that enough to establish this type of connection, invite children to hold up their hands with forefingers linked to give you the sign that they have made the personal connection. You don't need to give them time to explain. You may want to introduce the story, ask for "wonderings" and then give students time to turn to a neighbor and share a personal connection.

However, if they make more challenging connections with the world or another book, they may raise a hand and are allowed to explain the connection to the class. This encourages students to think at a higher level and to make connections beyond their own lives. Here are some books my teachers use annually which are rich in potential connections:

- *Koala Lou* by Mem Fox
- *The Relatives Came* by Cynthia Rylant
- *The Keeping Quilt* by Patricia Polacco
- *Knots on a Counting Rope* by Bill Martin, Jr.
- *Chrysanthemum by Kevin Henkes*
- *The Tenth Good Thing About Barney* by Judith Viorst
- *My Rotten Redheaded Older Brother* by Patricia Polacco
- *Alexander and the Terrible, Horrible, No Good, Very Bad Day* by Judith Viorst

What Did I Predict or Figure Out?

As you read aloud, stop at appropriate places when the protagonist is facing a problem or decision and ask students what they think the character will do next. Turn the page to see if they are correct. Think out loud as you read to students, verbalizing your own thinking as you read. You might think about a character's personality as revealed by her actions; you might make a connection to your life, the world, or another book; or you might wonder about the meaning of a word choice and why the author chose it.

Show students how to have a mental conversation with the author and illustrator. We used Suzanne Bloom's *A Splendid Friend Indeed* in a friendship unit and I thought aloud about all the clues the illustrator gave about the characters that aren't revealed in the text. Argue with the author: "I don't think that was a satisfying ending. How could we make it better?" By thinking aloud, you can exemplify what good readers think about as they read.

A couple of excellent examples for figuring things out are both books where pat answers don't work. In *Tomorrow's Alphabet by George Shannon*, students have to figure out why O is for acorn (it's tomorrow's oak tree). Each letter stands for something that will occur in the future. Shannon's *White Is for Blueberry* will get students thinking about how colors can represent objects that seem not to be that color. For example, "Pink is for crow" are the words below a sleek black bird. Think and guess, then turn the page. Did they predict that crows are pink when they are newborns? Blueberries are white before they begin to ripen.

It's not true that people use only ten percent of their brains (see the scientific mythbuster at faculty.washington.edu/chudler/tenper.html). However, it is true that students often do not use all the ways of thinking that are available to them when they read or hear stories. Make deliberate use of metacognition as you model reading and help students to take pleasure and be successful in their contacts with the written word. After all, a mind is a wonderful thing to use.

Examples of Wordless Picture Books

1. *1,2,3 to the Zoo* by Eric Carle. Penguin Group, 1998.
2. *Anno's Journey* by Mitsumasa Anno. Penguin Group, 1997.
3. *A Boy, a Dog, a Frog and a Friend* by Mercer and Marianna Mayer. Dial, 2003.
4. *A Boy, a Dog, and a Frog* by Mercer Mayer. Dial, 2003.
5. *The Boy, the Bear, the Baron, the Bard* by Gregory Rogers. Roaring Brook Press, 2007.
6. *Carl's Masquerade* by Alexandra Day. Farrar, Straus and Giroux, 1992.
7. *Changes, Changes* by Pat Hutchins. Aladdin, 1987.
8. *Chicken and Cat* by Sara Varon. Scholastic, 2006.
9. *Clementina's Cactus* by Ezra Jack Keats. Viking, 1999.
10. *Clown* by Quentin Blake. Henry Holt & Company, 1998.
11. *The Crocodile Blues* by Coleman Polhemus. Candlewick Press, 2007.
12. *Deep in the Forest* by Brinton Turkle. Penguin Group, 1992.
13. *Dinosaur!* by Peter Sís. HarperCollins, 2005.
14. *Do You Want to be My Friend?* by Eric Carle. Penguin Group, 1988.
15. *Flotsam* by David Wiesner. Houghton Mifflin Harcourt, 2006.
16. *Follow Carl!* by Alexandra Day. Farrar, Straus and Giroux, 1998.
17. *Free Fall* by David Wiesner. HarperCollins, 2008.
18. *Freight Train* by Donald Crews. Greenwillow Books, 1993.
19. *Frog Goes to Dinner* by Mercer Mayer. Dial, 2003.
20. *Frog on His Own* by Mercer Mayer. Dial, 2003.
21. *Frog, Where Are You?* by Mercer Mayer. Dial, 2003.
22. *Good Dog, Carl* by Alexandra Day. Aladdin, 1997.
23. *The Grey Lady and the Strawberry Snatcher* by Molly Bang. Simon & Schuster, 1984.
24. *Have You Seen My Duckling?* by Nancy Tafuri. HarperCollins, 1991.
25. *Home* by Jeannie Baker. HarperCollins, 2004.
26. *Island Dog* by Rebecca Goodale. Two Dog Press, 1999.
27. *Jack and the Night Visitors* by Pat Schories. Front Street, 2006.
28. *The Last Laugh* by Jose Aruego & Ariane Dewey. Dial, 2006.
29. *Museum Trip* by Barbara Lehman. Houghton Mifflin, 2006.
30. *Mysteries of Harris Burdick* by Chris Van Allsburg. Houghton Mifflin, 1996.
31. *One Scary Night* by Antoine Guilloppe. Milk & Cookies Press, 2007.
32. *Oops* by Arthur Geisert. Harcourt, 2006.
33. *Pancakes for Breakfast* by Tomie de Paola. Houghton Mifflin Harcourt, 1978.
34. *Peep!* by Kevin Luthardt. Peachtree Publishers, 2003.
35. *Picturescape* by Elisa Gutierrez. Simply Read Books, 2007.
36. *Rainstorm* by Barbara Lehman. Houghton Mifflin, 2007.
37. *Re-Zoom* by Istvan Banyai. Puffin, 1998.
38. *The Red Book* by Barbara Lehman. Houghton Mifflin, 2004.
39. *Sector 7* by David Wiesner. Houghton Mifflin, 1999.
40. *Sidewalk Circus* by Paul Fleischman and Kevin Hawkes. Candlewick Press, 2007.
41. *The Silver Pony: A Story in Pictures* by Lynd Ward. Turtleback Books, 1992.
42. *Snow Sounds: An Onomatopoeic Story* by David A. Johnson. Houghton Mifflin Harcourt, 2006. (nearly wordless)
43. *The Snowman* by Raymond Briggs. Random House, 1986.
44. *Time Flies* by Eric Rohmann. Random House, 1997.
45. *Trucks, Trucks, Trucks* by Peter Sís. Greenwillow Books, 1999.
46. *Tuba Lessons* by Monique Felix. Creative Editions, 2009.
47. *Tuesday* by David Wiesner. Clarion Books, 1991.
48. *Un-brella* by Scott E. Franson. Roaring Brook Press, 2007.
49. *Up and Up* by Shirley Hughes. RHCB, 2007.
50. *Window* by Jeannie Baker. HarperCollins, 1991.
51. *The Yellow Balloon* by Charlotte Dematons. Boyds Mills Press, 2004.
52. *Yellow Umbrella* by Jae Soo Liu. Random House, 2002.
53. *You Can't Take a Balloon into the Metropolitan Museum* by Jacqueline Preiss Weitzman. Puffin, 2000.
54. *You Can't Take a Balloon into the Museum of Fine Arts* by Jacqueline Preiss Weitzman. Puffin, 2001.
55. *Zoom* by Istvan Banyai. Puffin, 1998.

					What do you know?
					Verify
					What do you wonder?
					Answer

Cicadas

What do you know?	Verify	What do you wonder?	Answer
They make noise by rubbing their wings together.		Why are they so noisy?	Males buzz to call females (p. 14)
They are good at metamorphosis.	pp. 19–20	Why are cicadas so scary?	
They come out in summer.		What do they eat?	Juice from trees and plants. (p. 10)
Only the girls make noise.	Incorrect. Page 14: The males buzz.	Are they poisonous to their enemies?	
		Were they around in dinosaur days?	

Using Free Online Reference Tools • Library Lessons •

by | Karen Larsen (a.k.a. Anita Answer)   Grades 4–6

"I need to know how to translate this phrase into English."

"I need a map of Denver."

"I need to know how to spell 'albatross'—and just what is an albatross anyway?"

"I need another word for 'confused.'"

I swear I should change my name to Anita some days ("I need a …"). Of course being considered the font of all information is one of the job perks of being a librarian. Even if we don't know the answer to a question, we know where to find it. As school librarians, however, one of our tasks is to give students the skills they need to determine the best place to look for the information they need. After teaching them how to use the print sources available to them, it is also vital to familiarize them with online reference tools that they might need to access in the school library or at home, when print reference tools are not available.

Note: Be sure to familiarize yourself with the online resources before demonstrating to the class.

Lesson 1—Exploring Online Reference Tools: Part 1

Time Required: 30–35 minutes

Objectives
Students will take on the role of travel planners as they learn how to use the dictionary, thesaurus, and components of an online reference desk. They will also gain experience using MapQuest.

Materials
- Exploring Online Reference Tools: Part 1 worksheet (see page 74)
- computers with Internet access
- pencils

Procedure
1. Demonstrate for students how to access the virtual reference desk (www.infoplease.com).

2. Ask students for reasons a person would visit this site. (*Homework, writing a report, curiosity to learn new information, etc.*)

3. Demonstrate how to use the dictionary, thesaurus, and atlas. Then go to MapQuest (www.mapquest.com) and model how to use the site.

4. Explain that another time you might use this site, along with other online reference sites, is when you are planning a vacation. Trips run more smoothly when you plan ahead of time.

5. Either singly or in pairs, have students visit the sites listed and complete the worksheet.

6. Have students share what they found. Identify correct answers.

Answer Key: Exploring Online Reference Tools Part 1

1. Search Results: philidelphea
   Did you mean: philadelphia
   No documents found

2. Philadelphia/current Web definition

3. Possible answers: Autonomy Bell, Independence Bell, Freedom Bell, etc.

4. Camden (New Jersey); New York

5. Liberty Bell—Market Street between Fifth and Sixth Streets, Philadelphia, PA; 215-597-8974

Lesson 2—Exploring Online Reference Tools: Part 2

Time Required: 30–35 minutes

Objectives
Students will take on the role of travel planners as they learn how to use the dictionary, thesaurus, and components of an online reference desk.

Materials
- Exploring Online Reference Tools: Part 2 worksheet (see page 75)
- computers with Internet access
- pencils

Procedure
1. Review how to access the www.infoplease.com virtual reference desk.

2. Briefly review the dictionary, thesaurus, and atlas sections of this site.

3. Demonstrate how to use the almanac and encyclopedia sections of this site. Point out that the almanac covers quick, short facts, while the encyclopedia contains in-depth articles.

4. Either singly or in pairs, have students visit the sites listed and complete the worksheet.

5. Have students share what they found. Share correct answers.

Answer Key: Part 2

1. The City of Brotherly Love

2. Answers will vary.

3. Similar—both contain facts about the city. Different—the encyclopedia has more in-depth information.

Lesson 3—Exploring Additional Reference Sites

Time Required: 30–35 minutes

Objectives
Students will explore and become familiar with a variety of online reference sites. They will evaluate sites, considering ease of use, amount of advertising, interesting features, and other criteria.

Materials
- Exploring Additional Reference Sites worksheet (see page 76)
- computer with Internet access
- pencils

Procedure

1. Demonstrate how to access Fact Monster at www. factmonster.com.

2. Ask the students what they like about the layout of the site. Is it interesting to look at? Easy to use? What types of reference tools does it contain? When would you use this site? What do you like about it? What could be improved? Explain that finding information on different pages of a Web site by following instructions and clicking on tabs or links is called "navigating."

3. Discuss the advertising on the site. Why are there ads on the site? *(Answer: Web sites cost money to produce, put on a server, maintain, and to update. The site charges advertisers to post their ads, or advertisers pay the site each time a user clicks on its ad. There are online reference tools that do not contain ads, but they charge users subscription fees to access all parts of the site.)*

4. Either singly or in pairs, have students visit the sites listed and complete the worksheet.

5. Have students share what they found. Identify correct answers.

Answer Key: Part 3

Answers will vary, but should address ease of use, layout, and types of tools available on the site.

Lesson 4—Choosing the Right Reference Tool: A Quiz

Time Required: 30–35 minutes

Objective

The students will test their knowledge of online reference sites by taking a quiz that is constructed in a similar manner to state accountability tests.

Materials

• Choosing the Right Reference Tool: A Quiz (see page 77)

• computers with Internet access

• pencils

Procedure

1. On state tests, students need to fill in the bubbles on the answer sheet correctly. Demonstrate how to trace around the circle of the correct answer and fill it in. A computer-scoring machine will not count a check mark as correct. This is a great time for students to practice their bubbling-in technique.

2. Show the students how to eliminate the answers they know are incorrect to improve their odds at choosing the correct answer.

3. Either singly or in pairs, have students complete the quiz. For questions 6 and 7, they will need Internet access. These two questions are designed to allow the students to use higher level thinking skills of analysis and evaluation.

4. Review correct answers and have students share their responses to questions 6 and 7.

Exploring Online Reference Tools: Part 1

You are planning a family vacation and you turn to the Internet to help you plan the best trip ever. You know a successful trip takes a lot of forethought, and you are ready for the challenge!

1. It is important to know how to properly spell your destination city. You want to visit the Liberty Bell and you think the city is spelled "Philidelphea." Go to www.infoplease.com. Click on the dictionary. Enter "Philidelphea" in the search box. What result did you get?

   _____

   _____

   _____

2. What is the proper spelling of the city's name? _____
   Click on the suggestion. What does the definition say? _____

   _____

   _____

3. Thinking about the Liberty Bell has you wondering what other similar names the bell could have been given. Click on the thesaurus and type in "liberty" in the search box. Read the suggestions. If you were going to rename the Liberty Bell, what other name could you give it that has a similar meaning? _____

4. It would be helpful to see this city on a map. Click on atlas. You'll see a map of the world.
   • Click on North America.
   • Click on the United States.
   • Click on Pennsylvania (PA).
   • A map will display. Name a city that is near Philadelphia. _____
   • What state is directly north of Pennsylvania? _____

5. Now go to www.mapquest.com. Click on "Find It." Under "What," type in "Liberty Bell." Under city, type "Philadelphia." Under state, type "PA." Where exactly is the Liberty Bell located? (Read all the choices! Remember, you want the Liberty Bell—not a business.) Is there a phone number for the site?

   _____

   _____

   _____

Exploring Online Reference Tools: Part 2

Now that you know how to spell "Philadelphia," and you know where it is located, it's time to learn more about your vacation destination.

1. Go to www.infoplease.com. Click on almanac and type "Philadelphia" in the search box.
   • Click on the first response, Philadelphia, PA.
   • Read the entry. What is the nickname of the city? _____
   _____

2. List two interesting facts about Philadelphia.
   _____
   _____
   _____
   _____
   _____
   _____
   _____

3. Now click on encyclopedia and type "Philadelphia" in the search box. Next, click on "Philadelphia, city, United States." Read the introductory paragraph. Then click on "Institutions and Landmarks" and "History." Read each entry. Based on what you read:

   • How are the almanac and the encyclopedia similar?
   _____
   _____
   _____
   _____

   • How are the almanac and the encyclopedia different?
   _____
   _____
   _____
   _____

Exploring Additional Reference Sites

There are many great online reference desks. Visit each site and evaluate it. What do you like about the site? What do you think would make it better?

Fact Monster • www.factmonster.com

Is it easy to use? _____ Are there advertisements? _____

What types of reference tools does it contain? _____

Why or when would you use this site?_____

Is the content correct and easy to navigate? _____

The Kid's Space at the Internet Public Library • www.ipl.org/kidspace/browse/ref0000

Is it easy to use? _____ Are there advertisements? _____

What types of reference tools does it contain? _____

Why or when would you use this site?_____

Is the content correct and easy to navigate? _____

The Library Spot • www.libraryspot.com

Is it easy to use? _____ Are there advertisements? _____

What types of reference tools does it contain? _____

Why would you use this site? _____

Is the content correct and easy to navigate? _____

Refdesk.com • www.refdesk.com

Is it easy to use? _____ Are there advertisements? _____

What types of reference tools does it contain? _____

Why or when would you use this site?_____

Is the content correct and easy to navigate? _____

Yahoo! Reference • education.yahoo.com/reference

Is it easy to use? _____ Are there advertisements? _____

What types of reference tools does it contain? _____

Why or when would you use this site?_____

Is the content correct and easy to navigate? _____

Choosing the Right Reference Tool: A Quiz

You know you need information, but where is the best place to look? Take the following quiz and then discuss your answers with a partner.

1. You want to know how to correctly spell the name of the continent Australia. Which is the best online reference tool to use?
    - online thesaurus
    - online dictionary
    - online encyclopedia
    - online almanac

2. You would like to know some simple interesting facts about Australia. Which is the best online reference tool to use?
    - online thesaurus
    - online dictionary
    - online encyclopedia
    - online almanac

3. You are writing a report about Australia and you need another word for "outback." Which is the best online reference tool to use?
    - online thesaurus
    - online dictionary
    - online encyclopedia
    - online almanac

4. Your teacher wants you to draw a map of Australia and label the major cities. Which is the best online reference tool to use?
    - www.MapQuest.com
    - online reference desk
    - online encyclopedia
    - online atlas

5. You are very interested in learning more about the history of Australia. Which is the best online reference tool to use?
    - www.MapQuest.com
    - online reference desk
    - online encyclopedia
    - online almanac

6. Visit yahooligans.yahoo.com. Check out three different areas of this site. What did you visit and how and when would you use this site in the future?

    _____

    _____

    _____

    _____

    _____

7. Visit the following Web sites. Which of these additional online reference tools is your favorite?
    - www.weather.com
    - www.freetranslation.com
    - www.holidays.net
    - www.rudimentsofwisdom.com

    Why was it your favorite?

    _____

    _____

    _____

    _____

    _____

Poetry Pizzazz

• Library Lessons •

by | Judith Snyder

Grades K–2, 3–5

Highlight your library's poetry section and awaken children to the beauty of our language. Engage them in the cadence of words that trip teasingly off the tongue. Let them feel the beat of the earth reaching into their hearts. Make poetry come alive through immersion in the sound and rhythm of words.

The following student activities encourage physical, visual, and auditory involvement with poetry. Most can be modified for any grade level by choosing poems of appropriate complexity. The Teacher Collaboration Ideas provide ways to encourage teachers to use your library's poetry section and your resource talents.

All of these activities can be taught in isolation, but the biggest impact on student learning is made when lessons are planned collaboratively or team-taught with the classroom teacher. When adults model their love of and excitement about poetry, students respond with enthusiasm. Circulation soars and smiles abound! Note: Poems mentioned throughout this lesson are tied to their source books in the bibliography at the end.

Student Activities

Feel the Beat
Grade Levels: K–1
Objective
To develop understanding of the rhythm in poetry

Younger students enjoy moving to poems. Simple gestures actively engage early readers. Choose a simple poem like Beatrice Schenk de Regniers' "Keep a Poem in Your Pocket" or Dennis Lee's "Alligator Pie," "Little Bird" (reprinted on page 82), or others from *Pictures and Poetry* by Bunchman and Briggs. Write the poem on chart paper or display it on an overhead projector. Read the poem aloud once. Invite the group to read one stanza with you. Share simple

movements that illustrate what is happening in the poem. Read the stanza aloud with the movements before going on to additional stanzas. Give a copy of the poem to the classroom teacher to promote carryover into the classroom. Better yet, teach this together.

Experience Onomatopoeia
Grade Levels: 3–5
Objectives: To introduce the idea that the rhythm of words in a poem can copy a sound, and to develop reading fluency and expression

Sharing poetry in a reader's theater setting provides an authentic reason for reading practice that promotes fluency. Choose ten poems and allow students time to practice reading them aloud. For variety, assign different numbers of students to each poem. Some poems can be read in unison or split by stanzas or lines. Highlight specific poets like A. A. Milne, David McCord, or Karla Kuskin, or focus on a theme like family or weather. Nursery rhymes are also a great source and you don't have to worry about copyright.

Making Connections
Grade Levels: 3–5
Objective
To match poems to paintings and analyze similarities

Use famous art prints from calendars or your art teacher's collection and display them on a wall. Make copies of some classic poems, and laminate them for student use. The task is to read the poems and study the pictures to find commonalities between the two. Students identify poem/painting pairs that relate to each other; then write a few sentences explaining why they think the two fit together. Monet or O'Keefe prints work well in the spring, coupled with poetry by Eve Merriam or Christina Rossetti. During February, you may highlight famous African American painters like Romare Bearden, Horace Pippin, and Jacob Lawrence, contrasting with poetry by Langston Hughes or Nikki Giovanni. Find additional art and poetry couplings in Pictures and Poetry by Bunchman and Briggs.

Teacher Collaboration Ideas

Integrate poetry school-wide and year-round. The more poetry is integrated with ongoing curriculum units, the less intimidating it becomes. Anticipate upcoming units and give teachers poems or anthologies on the topic ahead of time. After teachers gain experience embedding poetry in the curriculum, they will continue to ask for quality poems. For example, Paul Fleischman's Newbery-winning *Joyful Noise: Poems for Two Voices* (HarperCollins, 2004) makes a science unit on insects buzz with excitement, and *Rough, Tough Charley* by Verla Kay (Tricycle Press, 2007) might fit well in a history lesson about the heyday of the American west. Here are more ideas to get you started.

Power Poems
Collaborate with classroom teachers when they teach descriptive writing techniques. Provide poems that illustrate literary devices. Here are a few suggestions:

Alliteration
- "Dusk" by Paul Fleischman
- "maggie and milly and molly and may" by e. e. cummings
- "Silver" by Walter de la Mare

Simile
- "Autumn Thought" by Langston Hughes
- "Rain Sizes" by John Ciardi
- "Song" by Michael Stillman

Metaphor
- "Fog" by Carl Sandburg
- "Taking Turns" by Norma Farber
- "Winter Morning" by Ogden Nash

Onomatopoeia
- "Clock" by Valerie Worth
- "The Pickety Fence" by David McCord
- "The Tree Frog" by John Travers Moore

Students who show understanding of the literary devices can search for poems containing them. This is a difficult task; it can be simplified by steering students to appropriate page ranges within an anthology. These poems can be shared with the class or displayed on a bulletin board.

Poetry Place

Produce a movie of students reciting or dramatizing poems. Use videotape or a video-editing program to create a forum where students can see themselves perform on T.V.—a highly motivating tool to engage reluctant poetry readers. If your school possesses the ability to broadcast live or via videotape recordings, use this capability to promote poetry. If not, produce a videotape to circulate among classrooms.

My school developed a weekly pre-taped segment we called Poetry Place. It is broadcast right after the announcements. Students of all ages were encouraged to recite memorized poems using simple gestures, props, or theatrics to create interesting presentations. Students signed up for weekly taping sessions. If the presentation needed additional practice, students received tips and were encouraged to sign up for tryouts again.

Since the first group sets the tone and expectations for the poetry presentations, you may want to pre-select students with a dramatic flair. Spend extra time with them practicing and providing presentation tips.

Useful presentation pointers:

- Speak clearly and slowly so the poem can be understood

- Use simple gestures that go with the poem

- Consider the poem's phrasing in order to recite it smoothly

- Modify the pace to fit the mood of the poem

- Use expression and inflection to avoid a singsong or monotone delivery

Give students anthologies and allow time to find the right poem. Students may present individually or in groups of any size. Invite classroom teachers to involve whole classes in filming individual poetry recitations or choral reading.

If you have a large population of foreign language speakers, collaborate with the ELL teacher to encourage students to share favorite poems or nursery rhymes from their first languages and cultures. Even though English speakers can't understand the words, the beauty of the languages still sings—and the ELL students proudly display language proficiency in their native tongues.

Video-editing Hints

In a video-editing program, create templates of several introductory and ending frames with titles and music that can be reused or updated with each Poetry Place Movie. Delete the footage of the previous performers and insert the new frames. The template can be updated to share information about tryouts or to give pointers about developing presentations. When the movie is completed, format it to share on your school network. Note: After the initial creation of the movie template at the beginning of the year, follow-up movies can be completed in as little as thirty minutes from initial taping to finished product.

If you don't have digital editing capabilities, use a video camera. Create posters that can be used as title frames for the beginning and end of the movies. Film the poster for a few seconds before taping student performances. Circulate the tape throughout the school for viewing. It isn't as easy to edit the clips, but the extra effort pays off in student smiles.

Why Memorize Poetry?

There is a difference between memorizing facts and memorizing a poem. In her book *Whisper and Shout: Poems to Memorize,* Patrice Vecchione says it beautifully: "The way to really know a poem, to befriend it, is to learn it by heart. Then, it's yours for always. You can take it wherever you go, and don't have to worry about losing the paper it was written on. To remember a poem you have to really read it, notice its details, the sounds it makes in your mouth, where it takes you in your imagination. Through memorizing poems you develop your ability to observe and remember the details of life. The poems then influence who you are and who you will become."

Note: Not all poems in all anthologies are suitable for children. Be sure to screen poems not mentioned in this article before sharing them with students.

Bibliography

- *All the Small Poems and Fourteen more* by Valerie Worth. Farrar, Straus and Giroux, 1996. (Contains "Clock.")

- *The Best of Ogden Nash* by Ogden Nash. Ivan R. Dee, 2007. (Includes "Winter Morning.")

- *The Bill Martin, Jr. Big Book of Poetry* edited by Bill Martin, Jr. Simon & Schuster, 2008. (Includes "Taking Turns.")

- *The Dream Keeper and Other Poems* by Langston Hughes. Knopf, 1994. (Includes "Autumn Thought.")

- *I Am Phoenix: Poems for Two Voices* by Paul Fleischman. HarperCollins, 1989. (Includes "Dusk.")

- *I'm Still Here in the Bathtub* by Alan Katz. Margaret K. McElderry Books, 2003.

- *Joyful Noise: Poems for Two Voices* by Paul Fleischman. HarperCollins, 2004.

- *Knock at a Star: A Child's Introduction to Poetry* edited by X. J. Kennedy and Dorothy M. Kennedy. Little, Brown and Company, 1999. (Includes "The Pickety Fence.")

- *Pictures and Poetry* by Janis Bunchman and Stephanie Briggs. Davis Publications, Inc., 1994. (Includes "This Is My Rock.")

- *Poetry by Heart* by Liz Attenborough. Scholastic, 2001. (Includes "Until I Saw the Sea," "River in Winter," and "Sidewalks.")

- *The Random House Book of Poetry for Children* by Jack Prelutsky. Random House, 1983. (Includes "Alligator Pie," "maggie and milly and molly and may," "Silver," "Song," and "Fog.")

- *Rough, Tough Charley* by Verla Kay. Tricycle Press, 2007.

- *20th Century Children's Poetry Treasury* by Jack Prelutsky. Knopf, 1999. (Includes "Alligator Pie," "Rain Sizes," and "Fog.")

- *Whisper and Shout: Poems to Memorize* by Patrice Vecchione. Cricket Books, 2002.

Theme-Related Anthologies:

- *Brothers and Sisters: Family Poems* edited by Eloise Greenfield. Amistad, 2008.

- *Hand in Hand: An American History through Poetry* by Lee Bennett Hopkins. Simon & Schuster, 1994.

- *Lives: Poems about Famous Americans* by Lee Bennett Hopkins. HarperCollins, 1999.

- *Omnibeasts: Animal Poems and Paintings* by Douglas Florian. Harcourt Children's Books, 2004.

- *Weather: Poems for All Seasons* by Lee Bennett Hopkins. HarperTrophy, 1995.

- *Winter Poems* by Barbara Rogasky. Scholastic, 1999.

Online References
For Reader's Theater techniques and background:

- www.readingonline.org/electronic/carrick/

- www.scriptsforschools.com/68.html

- www.loiswalker.com/catalog/teach.html

The Song of the Track

by David McCord

Clickety-clack,
Wheels on the track,
This is the way
They begin the attack:
Click-ety-clack,
Click-ety-clack,
Click-ety, clack-ety,
Click-ety
Clack.

Click-ety-clack,
Over the crack,
Faster and faster
The song of the track:
Clickety-clack,
Clickety-clack,
Clickety, clackety,
Clackety
Clack.

Riding in front,
Riding in back,
Everyone hears
The song of the track:
Clickety-clack,
Clickety-clack,
Clickety, clickety,
Clackety
Clack.

Little Bird

—Anonymous

Once I saw a little bird
Come hop, hop, hop.
And I cried, "Little Bird,
Will you stop, stop, stop?"

I was going to the window
To say "How do you do?"
But he shook his little tail,
And away he flew.

Genres

• Library Lessons •

by | Nancy Riemer Kellner

One of our roles as library media specialists is to help students recognize, understand, read, and appreciate a variety of literary genres. Whether this is driven by our states' frameworks or guidelines, teacher requests for collaborative lessons, or our own philosophy on the importance of exposing students to different kinds of literature, the teaching of genre is a critical element of the library media curriculum.

Concise, age-appropriate definitions of genres are crucial to your students' understanding of the concept itself as well as each individual type or sub-type. The lessons on the following pages can be used "as is" or modified for your specific needs. In addition, the handout on page 92 provides easy-to-understand definitions and characteristics of many sub-types of folklore. This handout was created by Charlene Schwartz, school librarian at the Doudna Elementary School in Richland Center, Wisconsin, and shared on the school librarians' listserv LM_Net.

Genres can be introduced to children in the primary grades using picture books. The mini-lessons in this article can be used singly, as a cohesive unit, or spread throughout the year as needed. The lessons can be piggy-backed onto other library lessons as well. For example, "Biography Beat" could be enhanced with another mini-lesson about alphabetizing or understanding the location and organization of biographies in the library. "Women in History" can be used in conjunction with Women's History Month. "This Could Really Happen" is a perfect opportunity to introduce an author study about Patricia Polacco. "Pile It On" is designed as a culminating activity for review and reinforcement.

Other titles can be substituted in each lesson to meet the curricular needs of your teachers, schools, and students. Have a selection of titles from the appropriate genre on display and available for borrowing at the end of each lesson. For a comprehensive list of suggested titles consult www. nancykeane.com/rl/ default.htm#Genres. Additional resources include *Children's Literature in the Elementary School* by Charlotte S. Huck et al (Brown & Benchmark, 1996), Los Angeles Public Library's Kids Path genre lists at www.lapl.org/kidspath/books/ genre/index.php, and Monroe County Public Library Booklists of Children's Literature at www.monroe.lib. in.us/childrens/booklists/children_booklists.html.

For children in intermediate grades, the study of genre is a review and expansion of what has been taught in the earlier grades. Teachers often assign book reports from a particular genre such as mystery, fantasy, or historical fiction. This is a wonderful opportunity to work cooperatively with classroom teachers by providing booktalks in support of assignments. The two lessons included here for older students are designed to be used as both reinforcement and assessment.

Biography Beat | Grades 2–3

Objective
To understand the definition and elements of biography and autobiography.

Featured Title
Author: A True Story by Helen Lester (Houghton Mifflin Books for Children, 1997)

Supplemental Title
Wilma Unlimited by Kathleen Krull (Sandpiper, 2000)

Activities
1. Write "BIO + GRAPHY" on the board. Explain that "bio" means life and that "graphy" means writing about. When they are put together they mean writing about someone's life. Stress that a biography is factual; in other words, **true** information about a **real** person.

2. Now write "AUTO" in front of "BIOGRAPHY." Explain that "auto" means self. An autobiography is a true story about the author's own life.

3. Read *Author*, explaining that even though the illustrations are cartoonish it is **not** a made-up story; it is a true story about Helen Lester's life.

4. Discuss elements of a biography such as information about the author's childhood, jobs, thoughts, feelings, failures, and successes. Brainstorm other elements that the author might have included such as family members, pets, education, travel, birth date and place, and hobbies. Remind students that a biography written about someone who has died would also include a reference to his or her date and place of death.

5. Encourage children to borrow biographies and autobiographies.

Women in History | Grades 2–3

Objective
To understand the definition of historical fiction and to be able to differentiate between historical fiction and biography.

Featured Title
Amelia and Eleanor Go for a Ride by Pam Muñoz Ryan (Scholastic, 1999).

Supplemental Title
Maria's Comet by Deborah Hopkinson (Aladdin, 2003)

Activities
1. Briefly define historical fiction as a story that takes place in history. Real historical figures may be featured, but parts of the story are made up.

2. Show children the cover of *Amelia and Eleanor Go for a Ride*. Ask if they know who Amelia and Eleanor were and why they were famous. If necessary, prompt for the answer by providing their last names (Earhart and Roosevelt).

3. Explain that even though they were real people who lived in history, this book is fictional. Tell the children that you will explain why it is fictional at the end of the story.

4. Read the book, pausing for discussion of confusing details or for student comments.

5. Point out why this book is classified as historical fiction—the dialogue is recreated; certain assumptions about what they ate and wore are made. Read the author's note to provide additional information as to why this book is fiction rather than biographical.

6. Explain that even though the book is fiction, the author includes many facts from history. When you read historical fiction you can learn about history while enjoying a story. If students want to learn more about Amelia or Eleanor, there are biographies about both women which tell the true stories of their lives.

7. Discuss the importance of research when writing historical fiction. Pam Muñoz Ryan used newspapers, books, and diaries to recreate this incident from history.

8. Encourage students to borrow historical fiction books.

Around the Campfire | Grades 2–3

Objective
To understand the concept of folklore (spoken stories passed down from generation to generation) and to recognize that every culture has its own folklore.

Featured Title
Arrow to the Sun by Gerald McDermott (Puffin, 1977)

Supplemental Titles
How Chipmunk Got His Stripes by Joseph Bruchac (Puffin, 2003); *Raven* by Gerald McDermott (Sandpiper, 2001)

Supplies:
- sticks and twigs
- lantern-type flashlight
- red, yellow, and orange tissue paper torn into small pieces

Activities
1. Have children sit in a circle. Allow them to build a "fire" using twigs and tissue paper. "Light" the fire with the flashlight.

2. Explain that long ago people didn't always understand why things in nature happened (the power of the sun; how animals looked; what causes rain, thunder, volcanoes, earthquakes, etc.).

3. People often made up tales to make sense of things that were puzzling or frightening. These tales were told to each other around campfires, but not written down like they are now.

4. Read or tell the selected stories.

5. Explain that these stories are just some of the kinds of folklore that can be found in the library. Briefly discuss other types such as fairy tales, fables, tall tales, and legends. Refer to the Let's Learn About . . . handout on page 92.

6. Show children places on your shelves where they can find folklore—in the picture books, fiction area, or nonfiction 398.2. Encourage them to borrow books from your folklore collection.

Listen for Clues | Grades 2–3

Objective
To understand that a mystery includes a problem to solve, clues and suspects. Students will act as detectives, using clues in text and pictures to hypothesize the title of the missing book.

Featured Title
Stella Louella's Runaway Book by Lisa Campbell Ernst (Simon & Schuster, 2001). Note that while this book is not technically a mystery, it is the perfect vehicle to teach the elements of a mystery.

Activities
1. Remind students that you have been learning about different genres of books during library class. Review previously studied genres (biography, historical fiction, folklore). Explain that there are more genres to explore, like mysteries, realistic fiction, and fantasy.

2. This week's genre is mystery. Brainstorm elements of a mystery. Expect or prompt for these answers:
   - characters who are suspects
   - characters who are solvers or detectives
   - a problem, puzzle, or crime to solve
   - clues
   - "red herrings" or false clues

3. As you introduce the book showing the cover and endpapers, remind students to look and listen carefully since they will be acting as detectives to solve a mystery.

4. Read *Stella Louella's Runaway Book.* Caution students not to call out once they have determined the title of the missing book. Encourage them to remember the clues to discuss at the end of the read-aloud.

5. As you near the end of the book, most students will have figured out the title of the missing library book and will be clamoring to call it out. Pause to allow them to share the answer and suggest that they can discuss the clues at the end.

6. When you finish, solicit a list of clues from students. For example, the chef at the restaurant loved the reference to porridge.

7. Reinforce the concept of the mystery genre by congratulating students on being good detectives and solving the mystery of the missing book!

8. Encourage students to borrow books from beginning mysteries series such as *Nate the Great, High Rise Detectives* and *Young Cam Jansen.*

This Could Really Happen |
Grades 2–3

Objective
To understand the concept of realistic fiction as a made-up story that could happen in real life. To understand that the characters are fictional but they behave in realistic ways and that the story takes place in the present.

Featured Title
Mrs. Katz and Tush by
Patricia Polacco (Random House, 2009)

Supplemental Title: *Song and Dance Man* by Karen Ackerman (Random House, 1992)

Activities
1. Review the genres that you have studied together. Repetition and review is important to reinforce genres.

2. Define realistic fiction. The key points are that characters and actions are realistic (not magical) and that the story takes place now, not in the past or the future.

3. Suggest that students listen for the author's theme or message while you read the book.

4. After reading, ask children to talk about the story's plot and the theme. If necessary, prompt responses about the theme, such as friendship, multicultural understanding, inter-generational understanding, love for a pet, etc. These are often themes in realistic fiction.

5. Have a selection of realistic fiction available for borrowing. Suggested authors for beginning chapter books include Johanna Hurwitz, Ann Cameron and Suzy Kline.

Fantastic Fantasy | Grades 2–3

Objective
To understand the concept of fantasy as a story that includes characters who do not exist in real life (such as wizards and fairies), events that could not really happen (such as time travel or magical transformations), or imaginary worlds. **Note:** Children at this age often cannot differentiate between fantasy and folktale. The key point to emphasize is that fantasy is an **original** story by the author, whereas folktales are **retellings** of stories that have been passed down through generations.

Featured Title
Sylvester and the Magic Pebble by William Steig (Atheneum, 2009)

Supplemental Title: *The Library Dragon* by Carmen Agra Deedy (Peachtree Publishers, 1994)

Activities
1. Define fantasy as a story that includes magical characters, magical events, or both.

2. Brainstorm types of characters or events that might be included in a fantasy (witches, wizards, fairies, trolls, unicorns, time travel, magic spells, talking animals).

3. Read *Sylvester and the Magic Pebble.* Discuss the theme of "being careful what you wish for." Have students suggest alternative wishes that Sylvester might have made.

4. As a closing activity, after students have selected and checked out books, call out various genres and have students line up by genre. Include informational books to accommodate borrowers of nonfiction.

Pile It On | Grades 2–3

Objective
To define and classify different genres using critical thinking skills and cooperative decision-making.

Supplies
- Twenty-four picture books representing the six genres studied plus extras for early finishers
- symbols/signs for each genre style (Create your own or enlarge the icons from the handout.)
- genre handouts from www.librarysparks.com

Activities
1. Review books that have been read or shared in the library during the genre study unit. Show each and remind students that each book is an example of a different genre—biography, historical fiction, folklore, mystery, realistic fiction, fantasy.
2. Remind students that "genre" means "type, category or kind" of literature. Explain that this is a way to categorize books similar to the way music is categorized as popular, folk, classical, jazz, etc.
3. Pass out the handouts.
4. Explain that students will work in groups to sort books by genre. Place the genre symbols/signs in six different locations in your learning space.
5. Have students count off by four and form groups. Instruct them to use the title, illustrations and text to place the book in the proper genre.
6. If a group finishes early, provide additional titles.
7. When all groups have finished, discuss rationales for each decision. If necessary, correct errors and explain why another choice would be better.

Fiction By Any Other Name...
| Grades 4–6

Note: This lesson requires a sufficient quantity of new books which do not yet have their genre spine labels affixed. If this is not possible, consider covering existing labels, using unlabeled cast-off book jackets or creating reproductions of book jackets.

Objective
To distinguish and classify different fiction genres.

Supplies
- genre classification spine labels (Available from Highsmith. Suggested categories: adventure, fantasy, historical fiction, mystery and science fiction. **Note:** Contemporary realistic fiction is not usually labeled.)
- spine label protectors
- reproductions of "Genres for the Intermediate Grades" (see page 91)
- selection of books without genre labels in a variety of fictional genres (one for each student)
- scrap paper
- pencils

Activities
1. Ask students for a definition of genre. Write the answers on the board. Prompt for "type," "sort," "category," and "kind" of literature or books. Demonstrate pronunciation of genre (zhän-rˊ). Explain that the word genre comes from the French language. Students enjoy hearing it pronounced and repeating it back with an exaggerated French accent.
2. To assist in understanding, use a sports analogy: Compare the concept of "Sports" to the concept of "Books." There is more than one category of "Sport" (baseball, football) just like there is more than one category of "Book." Next, compare fiction to baseball and nonfiction to football. Just as baseball players are divided into positions (pitcher, catcher, shortstop, center fielder), fiction is divided into genres. (Draw a web diagram on the board, showing fiction as the center of the web.) Brainstorm fiction genres; add suggestions to the web. Explain further that just as some baseball players can play more than one position, some fiction books may fall into more than one genre. Use *Holes*, by Louis Sachar, as an example of both realistic fiction and fantasy. Reinforce the analogy by similarly comparing nonfiction to football.
3. Inform students that they will identify genres for a new shipment of books. Explain how to find identifying clues in the title, book jacket illustration, text on the book jacket and Library of Congress Cataloging-in-Publication Data.

4. Choose one book and model the activity of determining genre and labeling. For example, if the title is *The Clue of the Missing...* it would by a mystery. If the characters wear historic costumes it would be historical fiction or nonfiction history. If the book jacket discusses aliens it would be science fiction. Show students how to align and affix genre labels to spines and cover them with spine label protectors.

5. Hand out the "Genres for the Intermediate Grades" sheet.

6. Have students count off by four and form groups. Pass out books and instruct students to use title, illustrations, and text to determine genre. Each student is to be responsible for one book, but decisions must be discussed with the group.

7. On scrap paper, have each student write his or her genre decision and two reasons for that choice.

8. Students then "apply" for a genre label by explaining to you why the genre was selected. If the choice is correct, he or she receives the appropriate classification label and a label protector to place on the spine. Remind the students that realistic fiction does not have a genre label.

9. Reward students with the privilege of borrowing these newly processed books. **Note:** I use this activity at the beginning of the year to introduce my student library volunteer program VISA (Very Important Student Assistants). Students are very excited about participating in authentic activities such as this one.

Genre Assessment | Grades 4–6

Objective
To analyze brief passages from literature in order to identify appropriate genres.

Supplies
- reproductions of "Genres for the Intermediate Grades" from page 91.
- reproductions of "Genre Assessment" from page 89.
- Genre Assessment answer key

Activities:
1. Review genre characteristics using the handout.
2. Read and discuss the instructions on assessment.
3. Have students complete the assessment either individually or in groups.
4. Upon completion and grading (optional), discuss the answers as a class. Have students explain the clues in the text that helped them to select the appropriate genre.

Genre Assessment Answer Key
1. f—Science Fiction (from *Aliens Stole My Body* by Bruce Coville)
2. h—Informational (from *Mummy Mysteries* by Brenda Z. Guiberson)
3. g—Biography (from *Colin Powell* by Rose Blue)
4. a—Adventure (from *Hatchet* by Gary Paulsen)
5. c—Historical Fiction (from *The Barn* by Avi)
6. d—Mystery (from *Mystery of the Plumed Serpent* by Barbara Brenner)
7. k—Poetry (from "Something Told the Wild Geese" by Rachel Field)
8. b—Fantasy (from *Which Witch* by Eva Ibbotson)
9. e—Realistic (from *Stranger in Dadland* by Amy Goldman Koss)
10. j—Oral Tradition (from *Rose Red and Snow White* retold by Ruth Sanderson)
11. i—Drama (from *Romeo and Juliet* by William Shakespeare)

Genre Assessment

Read the following eleven passages carefully. Each is from a different genre of literature. After each passage, fill in the blank with the letter of the genre that is the best fit. You may use your genre information sheet. If you are unsure about a passage, skip it and return to it at the end. Use each genre only once.

a. Adventure	e. Realistic	i. Drama
b. Fantasy	f. Science Fiction	j. Oral Tradition (folklore)
c. Historical Fiction	g. Biography	k. Poetry
d. Mystery	h. Informational	

_____ 1. It wasn't like I was going to starve; Edgar, the other half of the two-part alien creature my brain patterns had been merged with, was beaming energy into our body.

_____ 2. Mummies are real. They have been found in such diverse places as mountains, caves, ice and bogs, but they all have something in common . . . Mummies found in Alaska . . . were cleaned, dried and then protected by sea lion guts from water damage. Other mummies have been pickled in arsenic.

_____ 3. Colin Powell was born in Harlem in New York City on April 5, 1937. When Colin was still a child, his family moved to the South Bronx, another part of New York City . . . Colin Powell grew up to be a serious, strong military leader.

_____ 4. He could not believe the contents of the survival pack . . . a sleeping bag, an aluminum cookset, matches, a knife . . . an emergency transmitter. When the pilot rescued Brian he had been alone on the L-shaped lake for fifty-four days.

_____ 5. This leave-taking occurred in the spring of the year 1855, in the Willamette Valley, Oregon Territory . . . Father had been planting with the oxen in the west section when he took ill and collapsed.

_____ 6. The police rounded up the culprits and took everybody's name. Then they carefully collected all the treasure . . . and Michael and Elena did get the award.

_____ 7. Something told the wild geese
It was time to go.
Though the fields lay golden
Something whispered, "Snow."

_____ 8. It was a shock, of course. No one likes to think that their baby is going to grow up to be a wizard, and a black one at that . . . They changed their baby's name from George to Arriman (after a famous and very wicked Persian sorcerer).

_____ 9. Dad started to answer but the phone rang. I sat down in front of the TV while he talked. It was one of those shows where contestants scream their heads off to see who can act like a bigger jerk.

_____ 10. Once upon a time, a mother lived with her two daughters in a lonely cottage at the edge of a forest. Two rosebushes grew next to the front door, one with fiery red blossoms and the other bearing delicate white flowers.

_____ 11. JULIET: O Romeo, Romeo! Wherefore art thou Romeo?
Deny thy father and refuse thy name;
Or, if thou wilt not, be but sworn my love,
And I'll no longer be a Capulet.

ROMEO: [Aside] Shall I hear more, or shall I speak at this?

Genres for the Primary Grades

Historical Fiction

Real events are mixed with story that takes place in history.

Mystery

There is a problem or puzzle to solve with clues and suspects.

Folktale

Passed down by storytelling over the years;
there are often different versions.

Realistic Fiction

Modern story with events that could really happen.

Fantasy

Events, like magic or time travel, that could not really happen.

Biography

True stories about real people.

Genres for the Intermediate Grades

Found in the Fiction Section:

Adventure: Story often involves out-of-doors, survival, exciting journeys to interesting places; characters face challenges in order to triumph over difficult situations. Example: *Julie of the Wolves* by Jean Craighead George.

Fantasy: Events in story could not happen in real life; involves magic, wizards, and mythical characters. Example: *Harry Potter and the Sorcerer's Stone* by J. K. Rowling.

Historical Fiction: Story based on real historical events, times, or facts; characters may or may not be real people from history, but behave in realistic ways. Example: *Number the Stars* by Lois Lowry.

Mystery: Story revolves around a problem, crime, or mystery to be solved using clues; story is suspenseful; characters are solvers (detectives), suspects, and sometimes both. Example: *The Westing Game* by Ellen Raskin.

Realistic Fiction (also called Contemporary Realistic): Although the story is made up, characters behave in realistic ways; the story could really happen; setting is modern. Example: *Shilo* by Phyllis Reynolds Naylor.

Science Fiction: Made up events might possibly happen in the future based on scientific principles; space travel, robots, time travel, etc. Example: *A Wrinkle in Time* by Madeleine L'Engle.

Found in the Dewey Decimal Section:

Biographies: True stories about real people, living or dead, written by others. Example: *You Want Women to Vote, Lizzie Stanton?* by Jean Fritz.

Autobiographies: True stories about real people written by themselves. Example: *Boy* by Roald Dahl.

Informational: True books which include facts and information. Example: *Inside the Titanic* by Hugh Brewster.

Drama: Fiction written to be performed by actors for an audience; also known as a play. Example: Romeo and Juliet by Shakespeare.

Oral Tradition (Folktales/Folklore and Myths): Stories that were originally spoken and later written down. Story may change from version to version. This is a large category that includes fairy tales, fables, myths, legends, tall tales and epics. Example: *King Midas: the Golden Touch* by Demi.

Poetry: Stories written in verse; may or may not rhyme. Example: *Where the Sidewalk Ends* by Shel Silverstein.

Let's Learn About . . .

Genre	Folklore	Fable	Fairy Tale	Tall Tale/ Legend	Myth
Definition	A story that has been told orally and passed down through the years.	A short folklore story designed to give a message.	A folklore story that includes magical creatures or actions.	A folklore story based on historical truths or figures but has been expanded or exaggerated.	A traditional story of gods or heroes which tries to explain people, things, or events.
Characteristics		• Talking animals and/or elements of nature. • Usually one, two, or three characters. • Involves trickery. • Usually has just one problem. • Has a moral at the end.	• Often begins with "Once Upon a Time" and ends with "happily ever after." • Setting often in a town, castle, or forest. • Has good/nice characters and bad/mean characters. • Characters are often animals or royalty. • Problem often solved by magic. • Rules of three or seven. • Good is usually rewarded and evil is punished.	• A larger than life character with a specific job—based on a real person. • Exaggerated details that describe things as greater than they are. • Problem solved as a result of a test or struggle. • Problem might be solved in a funny way. • May include chants or repeated verses.	• Tries to explain elements of nature or life. • Has gods, goddesses, heroes, and unusual creatures. • People once believed myths were true, now they are • Many contain • Good is usually rewarded and punished. • Every culture its own collection myths.

The Mock Caldecott Unit

• Library Lessons •

by | Nancy Riemer Kellner **Grades 2–3**

Imagine the delight on my students' faces as I held up a handwritten letter addressed to them from Caldecott Honor author/illustrator David Shannon. Picture their reaction when I read aloud "Your teacher mentioned something called 'The Caldecott Award,' which I have heard of, but everyone knows the Peasleecott is the real honor!" Substitute a catchy name for Peasleecott inspired by your school's name and this experience could be yours.

For the past several years, second and third grade children at the Marguerite E. Peaslee School in Northborough, Massachusetts, have participated in a Mock Caldecott program as part of their Library and Information Literacy curriculum. The goals of this five-week unit range from exposure to Caldecott quality illustrations to defining distinguished artwork; from appreciation of various media and techniques to creating original awards.

Important as these learning goals are, it is the enthusiasm generated for the Caldecott Award that is the most rewarding. Not only will you increase circulation of Caldecott Award and Honor books, but you will create a buzz about the upcoming award announcement. Designed to be carried out during five library classes or visits (usually December and early January, prior to the announcement of the real Caldecott winner), this unit can be modified to meet your needs. However you present it, it is guaranteed to excite and empower your students to choose and enjoy high-quality children's literature.

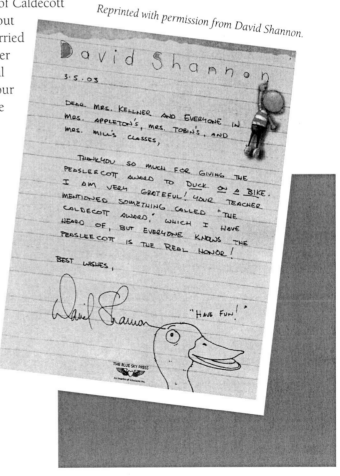

Reprinted with permission from David Shannon.

Pictures Are Worth a Thousand Words | Grades 2–3

Objective: To learn about different media and techniques and to appreciate how different media and techniques can set a tone in support of picture book text.

Supplies

- chart paper, white board or blackboard
- chalk or markers
- list of different media and techniques (see page 98)
- picture books representing various media and techniques
- Caldecott poster

Prepare in Advance

- Gather a selection of picture books illustrating different media and techniques (see suggestions on page 98). More suggestions are available at www.rif.org/art/illustrators_artwork.mspx.

- If you do not have a commercially produced Caldecott poster, create a mini-version by scanning the covers of the ten most recent Caldecott winners and mounting them on oak tag. Include a replica of the Caldecott Medal available at www.ala.org.

Activities:

- Show the Caldecott poster. Explain that the Caldecott Award is given to one book each year that has the "most distinguished" artwork. Explain that this means there is something special, different, and exceptional about the art. The pictures may not be the most beautiful, but they might be the most interesting. Emphasize that the award is based on how effectively the pictures relate to the words.

- Explain that next week students will choose the book they believe has the most distinguished artwork of the year. To do this, they will need to become art critics. In preparation for that important task, they will view many different types of illustrations.

- Have students brainstorm different types of artwork. Prompt by asking them to think about art class or trips to museums. Students will suggest both media (paint, crayons, colored pencils, etc.) and techniques (scratchboard, collage, prints,

etc.). Record answers on the board. Supplement student responses using the master list on page 98. Show examples of different media and techniques in pre-selected picture books. Point out how the pictures support the text by reading brief excerpts and noting the corresponding illustration. For example, the soft colored-pencil illustrations in *Song and Dance Man* (written by Karen Ackerman, illustrated by Stephen Gammell) give the story an old-fashioned feel.

- Conclude by reminding students that at the next class they will use their newfound skills to evaluate picture books and choose the previous year's Mock Caldecott. (The real Caldecott is announced in January for books published the previous year.)

Get Out the Vote | Grades 2–3

Objective:

- To evaluate artwork in picture books in order to select both a Peasleecott (Mock Caldecott) Winner and an Honor book.

Supplies

- Twenty-four to thirty-two picture books (copyright dated the current year), divided into four sets (see "Prepare in Advance" below)

- clipboards

- pencils

- scrap paper for notes

Prepare in Advance

- Gather picture books to be evaluated. Select books that are eligible for the Caldecott Award. According to the American Library Association Web site (www.ala.org): "The Caldecott Medal shall be awarded to the artist of the most distinguished American Picture Book for Children published in the United States during the preceding year. The award shall go to the artist, who must be a citizen or resident of the United States, whether or not he be the author of the text." The challenge to this step is to select twenty-four to thirty-two books from the thousands published during the year which are likely winners. Resources to help you choose include *School Library Journal,* other librarians, state library media associations, and the listserv LM_Net. (To join

LM_Net send an e-mail message to *LISTSERV@ LISTSERV.SYR.EDU*. In the first line of the message type: SUBSCRIBE LM_NET followed by your full name.)

- Divide the books into four sets. Aim for a mix of illustrative media and techniques as well as genres.

- Divide students into four sub-committees, keeping in mind learning and leadership styles. It is important to do this in advance so that class time can be spent evaluating books rather than forming groups.

Activities

- Review the previous lesson. Discuss the definition of "distinguished" and the importance of illustrations complementing the text of a picture book.

- Explain to students that they are now members of the very important Peasleecott Committee whose job it is to select both a Winner and an Honor book. Four separate subcommittees will make recommendations to the full committee.

- Explain that each subcommittee will evaluate six to eight books and choose the two most distinguished to present to the class.

- Have each sub-committee meet in a separate area. Provide clipboards, pencils, and scrap paper for notes. Instruct students to sample from the books, reading no more than a page or two of each. Groups may choose to look at the books together or browse individually and pass them around. Allow each sub-committee to find what works best for them. Each group must choose two books by consensus. These books will become finalists for the class vote.

- Circulate throughout the room. Allow time for thoughtful decisions, keeping in mind that a full class vote must follow. (I do this activity during a forty-minute library session. If you have a shorter period, the vote could wait until the following class.)

- Encourage groups that finish early to continue to browse and read books.

- Once each subcommittee has chosen two books, have students reconvene as a class. Have a representative from each group present their two titles. If time is critical, or with younger students, the librarian can present the finalists. Instruct the presenter to show two sample illustrations and briefly explain why his or her group thought the illustrations were distinguished.

- At the conclusion of the presentations, briefly review all eight contenders.

- Take a class vote, reminding students to vote for one title only. To encourage independent thought, conduct a "secret ballot." Show the book, have children close their eyes, raise a hand to vote, and then open their eyes after votes are counted. Repeat for each title. The two top vote-getters are the Winner and Honor Book, respectively. Have a run-off vote if necessary.

- Record winning titles on the board. Discuss if you have time.

- Conclude by informing students that the next lesson will be devoted to designing and creating awards for the Mock Caldecott winners. Remind students that the "real" Caldecott winner will be announced in January.

Note: Depending on the number of classes participating, you may want to choose school-wide winners as well. Do this by taking another vote after all classes have chosen their winners.

The 2003 Peasleecott Winner and Honor Books.

Award Design | Grades 2–3

Objective
To create Peasleecott (Mock Caldecott) Awards to be used in a display of winning titles.

Supplies
- award templates (see "Prepare in Advance" below)
- art supplies (crayons, markers, colored pencils, pencils)
- clipboards
- Caldecott poster (see "Pictures are Worth a Thousand Words" above)
- enlarged and laminated reproduction of Caldecott Medal

Prepare in Advance
- Photocopy the award template on page 99. Add your award name and school name. Photocopy one template for each student.

Activities
- Show the Caldecott Medal and pass it around.
- Explain that it is a replica (copy) of illustrator Randolph Caldecott's artwork and was created in his honor even though he never won the award himself.

- Discuss what might be suitable pictures or symbols for your Mock Caldecott Award. Brainstorm ideas (books, school, children reading, your school mascot, year of award, artwork from book, etc.). Discuss elements that should be part of the design—words, picture or symbol, year of award.

- Have students create designs in pencil and then add color.

- Explain that the mock awards may be used in a display or sent to the winning illustrators.

Listen to the Winners | Grades 2–3

Objective
To appreciate "award-winning" literature and analyze why these books were chosen as Mock Caldecott Winners.

Supplies
Winning titles from previous lessons.

Activities
This lesson is devoted to storytime and more in-depth discussion of the winning titles. It should be a relaxing celebration following three content-heavy lessons.

- Read aloud the Mock Caldecott Winner (and Honor book, if there is time).

- Discuss how artwork supports and advances the story.

- Compare the books to each other and/or other titles by the same illustrators.

Write to the Winners | Grades 2–3

Objective
To initiate correspondence with winning illustrator(s) using appropriate letter writing style.

Supplies
- copies of Mock Caldecott Winner and Honor books

- lined chart paper

- permanent markers

- correction tape

- Mock Caldecott Awards to accompany letter

- digital camera

Prepare in Advance
- Find the mailing address of your winning illustrator. You may write to the illustrator in care of the publisher of the winning book, or look for a mailing address on his or her official Web site.

Activities:
- Explain that classes can give the Mock Caldecott Award extra meaning by writing to the winning illustrators to inform them of this honor.

- Construct a letter as a class by brainstorming ideas and text. For example, you might explain the Mock Caldecott process, tell why students think the illustrations are distinguished, or thank the illustrators for their work.

- Act as scribe and draft a class letter on chart paper. Pay attention to proper letter-writing format and style; don't forget to include your return address.

- Have students sign first names to the letter. Use last initials as needed to distinguish among students.

- Enclose one Mock Caldecott Award chosen at random. (Students may decline this honor if they want their awards back.)

- Take a picture of the children and letter to include in the envelope.

- Explain that you will send the letter but that not all illustrators choose to respond and that the response may take some time. Anticipate six to twelve weeks.

The rewards of this unit go beyond appreciation of illustration techniques and quality artwork. In the years I have taught these lessons, we have heard back from Mary Azarian, David Shannon, Chris Soentpiet and Hudson Talbott. Our most exciting moment was when the 2002 Caldecott Winner was announced (*The Three Pigs* by David Wiesner) and we enjoyed the satisfaction of knowing that we chose it first! Despite the preparation involved, you will find that teaching this unit is as much fun for the librarian as it is for students.

Media and Techniques Used in Children's Book Illustrations and Suggested Titles for "Pictures Are Worth a Thousand Words"

Media/Techniques	Title	Author	Comments
Acrylics	*The Paperboy*	Dav Pilkey	
Charcoal	*Olivia*	Ian Falconer	
Collage	*Frederick*	Leo Lionni	
Colored Pencil	*Song and Dance Man*	Karen Ackerman	
Computer Generated	*Casey at the Bat*	Christopher Bing	
Cut Paper	*Hush!*	Minfong Ho	
Die Cut	*Joseph Had a Little Overcoat*	Simms Taback	
Gouache	*Arrow to the Sun*	Gerald McDermott	and pen and ink
Mixed Media	*Smoky Night*	Eve Bunting	
Oils	*Rapunzel*	Paul Zelinsky	
Pastels	*So You Want to Be President?*	Judith St. George	
Pen and Ink	*The Girl Who Loved Wild Horses*	Paul Goble	and watercolor
Pencil	*Make Way for Ducklings*	Robert McCloskey	
Photographs	*Jelly Beans for Sale*	Bruce McMillan	
Scratchboard	*Cendrillon*	Robert San Souci	
Stencil	*In the Small, Small Pond*	Denise Fleming	using homemade paper pulp
Watercolor	*Grandfather's Journey*	Allen Say	
Woodcut	*Snowflake Bentley*	Jacqueline Briggs Martin	

Award

Awarded to the finest example of an
illustrated children's book by the children of
_____ school.

Designed by: _____

Nonfiction—It Does a Brain Good

• Library Lessons •

by | Pat Miller   **Grades 3–5**

Grab a pen and paper and make a quick list of five books you most enjoy reading aloud to children. If you could only take five titles to a desert island to read to primary or intermediate grades, which would they be? Next, make a list of five of your favorite children's authors. Last of all, list five books or magazines you read most recently that were not written for children.

If you took the time to make these three lists (it's not too late, you can stop here and jot down your selections), examine your lists for fiction and nonfiction. Off the top of my head, here are my own lists:

Five Readalouds to Take to a Desert Island
1. *Bubba the Cowboy Prince* (Ketteman)
2. *Hatchet* (Paulsen)
3. *Anansi and the Moss-Covered Rock* (Kimmel)
4. *Sideways Stories from Wayside School* (Sachar)
5. *Junie B. Jones is a Beauty Shop Guy* (Park)

Five of My Favorite Children's Authors
1. Pam Muñoz Ryan
2. Joan Lowery Nixon
3. Christopher Paul Curtis
4. Gary Paulsen
5. Susan Stevens Crummel

Five Books/Magazines I've Read Recently
1. *Simple Scrapbooks* magazine
2. *Billy Straight* (Kellerman)
3. *National Geographic* magazine
4. *Picture Writing: A New Approach to Writing for Kids and Teens* (Suen)
5. *Traveling Mercies: Some Thoughts on Faith* (Lamott)

Without exception, my favorite children's authors and read aloud books were all fiction. But four of the five books/magazines I've read in the last two weeks were nonfiction. What does this say about the books we share with students and the lessons we teach in the library? If you looked over your lesson plans for the last few weeks, would you find that most of them centered on fiction? How much nonfiction have you booktalked recently? How many nonfiction authors have spoken to your students? How much nonfiction will our students read over a lifetime? Directions to their latest electronic game, the newspaper, requirements to earn a Scout badge, recipes, and textbooks—all are nonfiction. Standardized testing is emphasizing more nonfiction passages as well.

It's time to wean ourselves from our beloved fiction and make deliberate efforts to incorporate nonfiction into our read alouds, booktalks, and author visits. For lots of great author video clips, interviews, readings, biographies, and teaching guides, refer to www.TeachingBooks.net. Encourage your students to check out a fiction book for their right brain and a nonfiction book to exercise their left brain. Do the same in your lesson plans—and plan specifically to teach the very different skills needed to read nonfiction.

Becoming Aware of Nonfiction Features

Select a fiction book and two nonfiction books on the same topic. The nonfiction books should include a simple book and a more difficult book. All should be large enough for children to see while seated on the floor at your feet. Examples include:

Fiction:
- *Punia and the King of Sharks: A Hawaiian Folktale*

Nonfiction:
- *Sharks*, easy
- *Life-Size Sharks and Other Underwater Creatures* (more difficult)

Fiction:
- *Anansi the Spider: A Tale from the Ashanti*

Nonfiction:
- *Spiders*, easy
- *The Tarantula Scientist*, more difficult

Introduce, read, or booktalk your chosen books as time permits, using them to demonstrate the kinds of information available in each, and the presence or absence of features associated with nonfiction, like those listed on the Nonfiction Features Scavenger Hunt on page 103.

Then divide your class into three teams. Make four copies of the Scavenger Hunt form on page 103. Keep one form for your use in scoring team efforts. Cut the nonfiction features and their descriptions from the other three copies and paste them onto individual index cards. Make three color-coded decks of cards so each team has a complete, identifiable set. Seat teams in circles on the floor around a pile of nonfiction books. Be sure that each of the features listed shows up in at least one book in each pile.

Give each team a box or bag with the cards inside. At the signal, a member from each team pulls a card and reads it to his or her team. Then each team member takes a book and tries to find that nonfiction feature. When it is located, teammates check the answer and all raise their hands if they agree. The librarian or teacher verifies, and puts a star on the scoring sheet, in the column next to the feature for that team. The first team to find a designated number of features wins the game.

Nonfiction Keys Activity

Introduce these ideas about keys to nonfiction: We need keys to open doors, start the car, and help us get what and where we want. In a similar way, we can use information keys to help us get the things we want from nonfiction books. Hold up a ring with three large keys and explain that these keys are:

- **Visual Keys**—These keys help us get more information with our eyes. They show us information in images or graphic organizers like graphs or time lines.

- **Informational Keys**—These keys help us get information through written facts. They tell us information in words.

- **Organizational Keys**—These keys organize visual and written keys in ways that help us locate information throughout a book.

Again, form three teams. Give each a copy of the Nonfiction Keys worksheet on page 104. Explain that, with their team, students are to sort the keys onto key rings (into columns). Teams will decide together how to choose if they don't all agree on the best ring for a particular key. Some keys can fit on more than one ring. Teams should be ready to explain their choices.

Give students time to discuss and complete the worksheet. Go over the answers below. Anticipate lively discussion and give credit for any answers that are backed up with good reasons.

Suggested answers:
- **Visual Keys:** close-up, comparison, cutaway, font, graph, map, photograph, time line
- **Written Keys:** caption, chart, diagram, label, sidebar
- **Organizational Keys:** appendix, bibliography, glossary, index, table of contents

Sources of More Nonfiction Lessons

Awareness and knowledge of terms are the first steps in locating and using nonfiction features. Enlarge the descriptions from the Nonfiction Features Scavenger Hunt form to a size you can post in your library

or classroom to use when discussing informational books. Stress the importance of reading nonfiction slower and with more attention to the additional features like font, captions, charts, etc. For more activities on teaching nonfiction reading skills, refer to some of the books below. You will find lesson plans, background knowledge, strategies for teaching, Kathleen Baxter's newest nonfiction booktalks, and a book on presenting nonfiction authors.

- *Exploring the Literature of Fact: Children's Nonfiction Trade Books in the Elementary Classroom* by Barbara Moss. Guilford Publications, 2002.

- *Gotcha Covered! More Nonfiction Booktalks to Get Kids Excited About Reading* by Kathleen A. Baxter and Michael Dahl. Greenwood Publishing Group, 2005.

- *Nonfiction in Focus: A Comprehensive Framework for Helping Students Become Independent Readers and Writers of Nonfiction, K–6* by Janice V. Kristo and Rosemary A. Bamford. Scholastic, 2004.

- *Nonfiction Matters: Reading, Writing and Research in Grades 3–8* by Stephanie Harvey. Stenhouse Publishers, 1998.

- *Popular Nonfiction Authors for Children: A Biographical and Thematic Guide* by Flora R. Wyatt, Margaret Coggins, and Jane Hunter Imber. Libraries Unlimited, 1998.

- *Reading with Meaning: Teaching Comprehension in the Primary Grades* by Debbie Miller. Stenhouse Publishers, 2002.

- *Strategies that Work: Teaching Comprehension to Enhance Understanding* by Stephanie Harvey. Stenhouse Publishers, 2000.

- *Teaching Students to Read Nonfiction* by Alice Boynton and Wiley Blevins. Scholastic, 2003.

- *Teaching Students to Read Nonfiction, Grades 2–4* by Alice Boynton and Wiley Blevins. Scholastic, 2004.

Bibliography

- *Anansi and the Moss-Covered Rock* retold by Eric A. Kimmel. Holiday House, 1988.

- *Anansi the Spider: A Tale from the Ashanti* by Gerald McDermott. Henry Holt & Company, 1987.

- *Billy Straight* by Jonathan Kellerman. Random House, 1999.

- *Bubba the Cowboy Prince: A Fractured Texas Tale* by Helen Ketteman. Scholastic, 1997.

- *Hatchet* by Gary Paulsen. Simon & Schuster, 1987.

- *Junie B. Jones is a Beauty Shop Guy* by Barbara Park. Random House, 1998.

- *Life-Size Sharks and Other Underwater Creatures* by Daniel Gilpin and Martin Knowelden. Sterling Publishing, 2005.

- *Picture Writing: A New Approach to Writing for Kids and Teens* by Anastasia Suen. Writer's Digest Books, 2002.

- *Punia and the King of Sharks: A Hawaiian Folktale* adapted by Lee Wardlaw. Dial, 1996.

- *Sharks* by Carol Lindeen. Capstone Press, 2005.

- *Sideways Stories from Wayside School* by Louis Sachar. HarperCollins, 1998, 1978.

- *The Tarantula Scientist* by Sy Montgomery. Sandpiper, 2007.

- *Traveling Mercies: Some Thoughts on Faith* by Anne Lamott. Knopf, 1999.

Nonfiction Features Scavenger Hunt

	Team 1	Team 2	Team 3
Appendix—gives additional information at the end of the book			
Bibliography—lists books and Internet sites used in the book			
Caption—explains a picture or photo in a phrase or sentence			
Chart—organizes information in columns and rows so it's easy to understand			
Close-up—shows details of an object			
Comparison—shows the size of something you don't know next to something you know			
Cutaway—removes part of the outside to show you the inside			
Diagram—explains parts of a whole using an outline of an object and labels			
Font—highlights what's important using letters in contrasting size, color, or shape			
Glossary—defines difficult or specialized words in the book			
Graph—shows numerical information so you can make comparisons			
Index —lists key words in the book and pages on which they are found			
Label—explains part of a picture			
Map—helps you locate where things are in the world using drawings			
Photograph—shows exactly what something looks like			
Resource List—suggests books or Web sites that give more information			
Sidebar—adds related information in a box next to the main text			
Table of Contents —tells the order of the topics in the book			
Time Line—shows events in the order in which they happened or will happen			

Nonfiction Keys

Team Name: _____ Teacher: _____

Discuss the following keys with your team. Use the nonfiction books to help you. Decide what kind of key each one is. Sort them onto the correct key ring by writing them in the appropriate columns.

appendix	cutaway	label
bibliography	diagram	map
caption	font	photograph
chart	glossary	sidebar
close-up	graph	table of contents
comparison	index	time line

Visual Keys	Written Keys	Organizational Keys

The Penultimate Peril

• Library Lessons •

by | Lynn Farrell Stover Grades 3–5

"The entire 100 section of a library is dedicated to philosophy and psychology, and so is the first story of our hotel, from the reception desk, which is labeled 101 for the theory of philosophy, to the concierge desk, which is labeled 175 for the ethics of recreation and leisure, to the couches over there, which are labeled 135 for dreams and mysteries, in case our guests want to take a nap or conceal something underneath the sofa cushions."

-Frank or Ernest explaining the organization of Hotel Denouement to the Baudelaire siblings

Story Synopsis

THE PENULTIMATE PERIL

Things continue to go awry for the three Baudelaire orphans in book twelve of A Series of Unfortunate Events. Upon picking the children up in a taxi at the Briny Beach, an emotional Kit Snicket drives them to the enigmatic Hotel Denouement. There she leaves them disguised as concierges with instructions to station themselves in the hotel and spy on the guests to try to determine who is friend and who is foe. They are also to prepare for a V.F.D. meeting that is to be held at the hotel on Thursday. While acting as flaneurs (people who quietly observe their surroundings), the children soon discover the unusual organization of the hotel. The building is arranged based on the Dewey Decimal system. For example, if you ventured into room 831 you would find a gathering of German poets! The

book serves as a review for the eleven that came before it and a set-up for the next one, the last scheduled for the series. Hence the "Penultimate" title.

Note: *While many students are familiar with the popular* A Series of Unfortunate Events *books, students need not have read the featured title to complete these lessons. The activities may be used as class instruction to individual students, cooperative learning groups, or as part of a learning center.*

Lesson 1: The Dewey Decimal System at the Hotel Denouement

The Hotel Denouement (*denouement* meaning conclusion, finale, the end) may be full of dangerous and bizarre people, but it is very well organized. One of the hotel's owners, either Frank or Ernest Denouement, explains it to the Baudelaire siblings. "The second story is the 200s for religion, and we have a church, a cathedral, a chapel, a synagogue, a mosque, a temple, a shrine, a shuffleboard court, and Room 296, which is currently occupied by a somewhat cranky rabbi." He continues to describe the hotel, which follows the Dewey Decimal system in its floor plan, telling the children, "You'll probably walk through every section of the hotel, from the astronomy observatory in Room 999 to the employees' quarters in the basement, Room 000."

Time Required: 25–30 minutes

Objectives

- Students will review the Dewey Decimal system.

- Students will participate in a creative problem solving activity using the Dewey Decimal System's classification structure as an organizational tool.

Materials

- Dewey Decimal system visual (page 108)

- What's the New Dewey Decimal Number? activity (page 109)

- writing tools

- optional: copy of *The Penultimate Peril* by Lemony Snicket to display

Directions

1. Prior to class, make a transparency of the visual and enough copies for your students.

2. Inform students that this lesson will concern the Dewey Decimal System, which is the method used to organize materials in most school libraries. You might read pages 62–64 in *The Penultimate Peril*, which describes how the Hotel Denouement is organized using the Dewey Decimal System.

3. Display and review the visual. Point out where the Dewey hundreds categories are located in your library.

4. Pass out the activity sheet. Students may work individually or in groups. Check as a group when students complete the task. *Possible Answers:* 1. 200s, 2. 500s, 3. 000s, 4. 300s, 5. 100s, 6. 600s, 7. 100s, 8. 600s, 9. 700s, 10. 900s, 11. 800s, 12. 400s. However, accept all logical responses, as the books described do not actually exist!

5. More information concerning the Dewey Decimal System and Melvil Dewey can be found at these Web sites: www.oclc.org/dewey, www.mtsu.edu/~vvesper/dewey.html, www.booktalking.net/books/dewey.

Lesson 2: Author's Alliteration Alert

Author Lemony Snicket loves to play with words. A Series of Unfortunate Events is full of acronyms, palindromes, and secret codes. The book titles themselves follow the same alliterative pattern, and often have double meanings. Students can have fun learning literary terms while suggesting additional titles that fit the pattern.

Time Required: 20–25 minutes

Objectives

- Students will be introduced to alliteration.

- Students will participate in a class discussion and activity applying word play to book titles.

Materials

- Author's Alliteration Alert! (page 110)

- transparency marker

- optional: copies of Lemony Snicket's books to display

Directions

1. Make a transparency of the visual prior to class.

2. Display the visual and discuss it with students.

3. Solicit possible titles and record them on the visual.

Lesson 3: Lemony's Library Lesson—Dewey Decimal Shelf Search

Students learn best by doing! Get them out of their seats and over to the shelves with a Dewey Decimal Shelf Search.

Time Required: 30–40 minutes

Objectives

- Students will review the Dewey Decimal System and the literary term alliteration.

- Students will discover the location in the library of specific groups of books.

Materials

- Dewey Decimal Shelf Search activity (page 111)
- writing tools

Directions

1. Prior to class, make a transparency of the activity sheet and enough copies for your students.

2. Tell students that Klaus Baudelaire, a character in Lemony Snicket's A Series of Unfortunate Events, is always looking for a book on the library shelf to help him solve a problem. This lesson is similar to what Klaus tries to do.

3. Display the transparency and discuss the content.

4. Give each student or group a copy of the activity sheet. Explain your expectations, such as putting books back on the shelves in order, respecting others, or using time wisely.

5. Inform students that they may not have time to complete the chart. Their scores will reveal how hard they worked.

6. At the end of the allotted time, have students return to their seats, calculate their scores, and share their book "discoveries."

7. Invite students to check out interesting books they discovered on the shelves during this activity!

The Dewey Decimal System

An American named Melvil Dewey devised the Dewey Decimal System in the late 1800s. This numerical system organizes the books in the library into ten categories of knowledge.

- **000s—General Works** [*Encyclopedias, Reference Books*]

- **100s—Philosophy** [*Philosophy, Psychology, Paranormal Phenomena*]

- **200s—Religion** [*Church History, Mythology, All Religions*]

- **300s—Social Sciences** [*Manners, Law, Folklore*]

- **400s—Language** [*Dictionaries, Foreign Languages*]

- **500s—Natural Science** [*Mathematics, Chemistry, Biology*]

- **600s—Technology & Applied Science** [*Inventions, Health*]

- **700s—Fine Arts** [*Art, Music, Crafts, Sports, Hobbies*]

- **800s—Literature** [*Poetry, Plays, Short Stories*]

- **900s—History** [*Geography, Biography, Travel*]

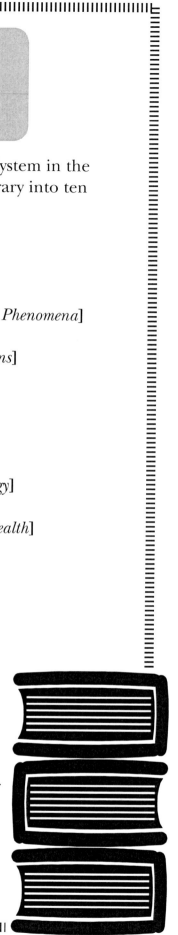

Note: Books of fiction could be cataloged using the Dewey Decimal number 813. However, because there are usually so many of these books, most libraries have a section just for the fiction books, which are organized alphabetically by the authors' last names.

What's the New Dewey Decimal Number?

Lemony Snicket has written many books about the miserable lives of the poor Baudelaire children, all of them fiction. What if these titles were not fiction? What Dewey Decimal number would you assign them so they could be easily located on the library's shelves? Using the chart below and the make-believe descriptions, decide what new category each title could be placed under. Be prepared to defend your choices.

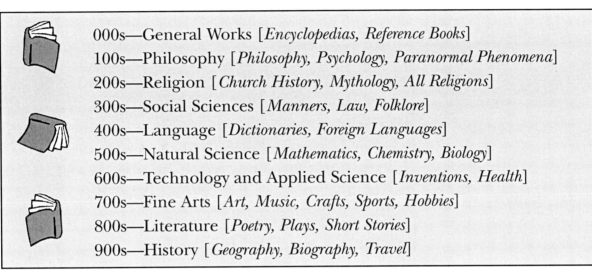

000s—General Works [*Encyclopedias, Reference Books*]
100s—Philosophy [*Philosophy, Psychology, Paranormal Phenomena*]
200s—Religion [*Church History, Mythology, All Religions*]
300s—Social Sciences [*Manners, Law, Folklore*]
400s—Language [*Dictionaries, Foreign Languages*]
500s—Natural Science [*Mathematics, Chemistry, Biology*]
600s—Technology and Applied Science [*Inventions, Health*]
700s—Fine Arts [*Art, Music, Crafts, Sports, Hobbies*]
800s—Literature [*Poetry, Plays, Short Stories*]
900s—History [*Geography, Biography, Travel*]

1. *The Bad Beginning*—What if this book was a Greek myth about Chaos and Oceanus and their role in the creation of the universe? _____

2. *The Reptile Room*—What if this book was about snakes and lizards? _____

3. *The Wide Window*—What if this was the title of an encyclopedia that described everything that could be seen from a very wide window? _____

4. *The Miserable Mill*—What if this book described the terrible working conditions during the industrial revolution that led to the creation of labor unions? _____

5. *The Austere Academy*—What if this book told of Plato's philosophy based on his deep thoughts and teachings? _____

6. *The Ersatz Elevator*—What if this book was about some of the crazy and ill-fated inventions that changed the world? _____

7. *The Vile Village*—What if this book contained the theory that Big Foot, Crop Circles, and UFOs may have one small nasty place in common? _____

8. *The Hostile Hospital*—What if this book was about the diseases discovered and the medicine made to cure them in a hospital during a horrible war? _____

9. *The Carnivorous Carnival*—What if this was a book of illustrations and instructions on how to make costumes for circus folk like clowns and jugglers? _____

10. *The Slippery Slope*—What if this was a book about the geography of the Andes Mountains? _____

11. *The Grim Grotto*—What if this was a book containing a collection of sad short stories? _____

12. *The Penultimate Peril*—What if this was a book about how to stay out of trouble by using grammar correctly? _____

Author's Alliteration Alert!

Lemony Snicket has completed the final book in A Series of Unfortunate Events. Each one except the last has an alliterative title. Alliteration is the repetition of beginning consonant sounds. Mr. Snicket starts each title with the word "The" and follows it with two words, usually an adjective and a noun. In the titles which follow the pattern, no letter of the alphabet is repeated. Using this knowledge, create an alternate title for the thirteenth book which fits the pattern. Tip: The letters D, F, I, J, K, L, N, O, Q, T, U, X, Y, and Z have not been used.

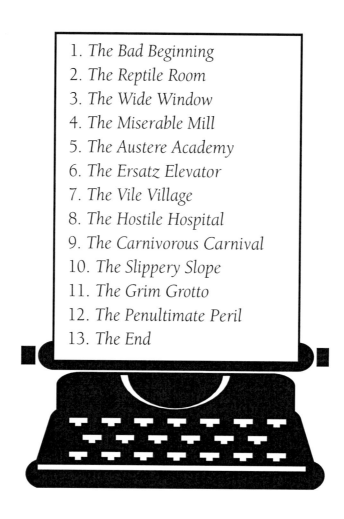

1. The Bad Beginning
2. The Reptile Room
3. The Wide Window
4. The Miserable Mill
5. The Austere Academy
6. The Ersatz Elevator
7. The Vile Village
8. The Hostile Hospital
9. The Carnivorous Carnival
10. The Slippery Slope
11. The Grim Grotto
12. The Penultimate Peril
13. The End

What might be good alternate titles for the thirteenth book if the series were going to continue?

1. _____

2. _____

3. _____

4. _____

5. _____

Dewey Decimal Shelf Search

Use strategy, skill, and speed to search your library's shelves and complete as much of the chart as you can in the allotted time. You'll earn extra points for books you find and select to represent a Dewey Decimal Group that have alliterative titles. (Alliteration is the repetition of beginning consonant sounds.)

Example

Dewey	Group	Title (10 points)	Author (2 points)	Alliterative Title (5 bonus points)
400–499	Language	Grammar is Great! Verbs are Vital!	Ruth Thompson	X

Dewey Numbers	Group	Title (10 points)	Author (2 points)	Alliterative Title (5 bonus points)
000–099	General Works			
100–199	Philosophy			
200–299	Religion			
300–399	Social Sciences			
400–499	Language			
500–599	Natural Science			
600–699	Technology			
700–799	Fine Arts			
800–899	Literature			
900–999	History & Geography			

SCORE:

Listed Titles _____ x 10 = _____

Listed Authors _____ x 2 = _____

Bonus Points _____ x 5 = _____

TOTAL POINTS

_____

Successful State Mini-Research

• Library Lessons •

by | Karen Larsen   **Grades 3–5**

Projects for All Learners!

All students can experience success with differentiated, collaboratively taught lessons. This set of lessons is an introduction to studying your home state. The skills and knowledge gained will help students with later instruction about state history and geography.

A differentiated lesson is designed to teach a group of students similar skills and concepts while ensuring that each student is challenged at his or her own level of instruction.

In addition to covering state history and geography standards, these lessons address a variety of research and literacy standards:

- Accessing information efficiently and effectively

- Locating information using an index and a table of contents

- Evaluating information critically and competently

- Writing a bibliography

- Using a variety of resources

- Using information accurately and creatively

- Reading to locate, select, and make use of relevant information from a variety of media, reference, and technological sources

- Creating a beginning PowerPoint® presentation

Lesson 1: Selecting Your Topic

Time Required: 30–45 minutes

Objectives
Students will discuss a variety of state topics for possible study.

Materials

- A transparency which you create listing many possible topics about your state that you have resources for in your library. It should look something like this, with at least ten options under each category heading:

CO Symbols	CO People	CO Places	CO Events
State Mammal: Big Horn Sheep	Molly Brown	Central City	The Gold Rush
State Seal	Zebulon Pike	Estes Park	Sand Creek Massacre
State Flag	Chief Ouray	Mesa Verde	The Dust Bowl
State Tree: Blue Spruce	Clara Brown	Denver	Ludlow Massacre

- Before beginning the lesson, pull books about state people, state places, state symbols, and state events. Place one topic in each tote and place one tote on each table. Label each tote: "(Your State)" Places, etc. Depending on class size and seating arrangements, you may have two tables studying each topic.

Procedure

1. Have students randomly sit at the tables.

2. Using the transparency, give a brief "commercial" for each category.

   - **Symbols:** Explain that it will be fairly easy to locate information; students will only have to use a few resources. They should like to draw details.

   - **People and the Places:** Explain that it will be a little more difficult to research these categories. Students will have to check several resources to pull the information together.

   - **Events:** Explain that this will be the most difficult, and is best for students who want a challenge. They will have to consult several resources, which may have different information. It will be their job to sift through the information and rewrite it in a way that makes sense.

3. Explain that students may choose which category and what item on the list they want to study, but teachers may offer guidance to help balance the groups and make sure everyone is successful.

4. Have students stand up and move to the side of the room. Ask those who are interested in studying a state symbol to raise their hands. The teacher will choose students who are most likely to be challenged and have success in this group. Students chosen to study a symbol will move to the symbol tables. Note: After doing this several times, I have found that students usually do a great job of selecting appropriately for themselves. Occasionally we have to say something like, "Bobby, I think you would do a great job in the State Places group. Would you consider joining them?" Occasionally, a student is adamant about studying a certain topic. I let him or her choose.

5. Continue in this manner choosing students for the people, places, and events tables.

6. Allow students time to peruse the books in their tote. Encourage them to pass the books around and quietly explore all possibilities. Ultimately, each student must choose a different topic.

7. With a teacher, explain how to have a group discussion to select topics. Point out that yelling things like, "I call Estes Park!" will not work. We are learning to discuss and compromise. Model something like this discussion:

Teacher: Wow, there are lots of great people to choose from. I am leaning toward either Molly Brown or Chief Ouray.

Librarian: I once read a book about the *Titanic,* so I was thinking Molly Brown would be interesting. When I was looking through the books though, I think I would also be interested in learning more about Emily Griffith.

Teacher: The more I think about it, if everyone else agrees, I would love to learn more about Chief Ouray.

Librarian: You know, I already know something about Molly Brown and I really do not know much about Emily Griffith, so I think I would like to study her.

Then walk around and listen in on the table discussions until everyone has made their choices. Record each topic that each student has chosen to study.

8. Demonstrate how to use a Table of Contents and an Index to find information. Give students sticky notes to mark their places in the books.

9. Allow the rest of the time for research. Before dismissal, ask students to share with their tablemates one interesting fact they have learned about their topic.

Lesson 2: Gathering Research—Parts 1 and 2

Time Required: Two or more class periods

Objectives
Students will research their topics using a variety of research tools.

Materials
- Category Worksheet Pages from pages 117-119; make copies of each category in a different color so you can see at a glance who is working on what

- one copy for each student of the State History Bibliography page template on page 116

- books in totes

- encyclopedia set

- computer with Internet access

- pencils

Procedure

1. Have students sit at their category tables.

2. Model how to find appropriate information and answer the questions on their worksheets. Advise them to skip questions if they get stuck, and come back to those later.

3. Show students how to find information in the encyclopedia and provide sticky notes to mark their places.

4. As students work, select a few at a time and help them locate information about their topics on the Internet.

5. Demonstrate how to create the bibliography.

6. As students finish answering the questions, have them move on to drawing pictures about their topics.

Lesson 3: Writing the Paragraph

Time Required: One class period

Objectives
Students will use their research to create a paragraph about their topic.

Materials
- Student category worksheets from Lesson 2
- transparencies of paragraph pages from each category worksheet
- pencils

Procedure

1. Using a transparency of the state symbol paragraph, model how to write a paragraph using information gleaned from research.

2. Quickly demonstrate the process for each of the other categories.

3. Give students time to write their paragraphs. Circulate and help as needed.

4. Have tablemates help each other edit their paragraphs with assistance from a teacher.

5. Take turns reading paragraphs aloud at each table.

Lessons 4 and 5: PowerPoint

Time Required: 1–2 class periods

Objectives
Students create PowerPoint® presentations using their completed worksheets.

Materials
- State Research PowerPoint® Category Slide Lists from page 120; provide each student with a copy of the appropriate category list
- State Bibliography template (page 116); make a copy for each student
- transparency of State Bibliography template
- completed student category worksheets from previous lessons
- computers

Procedure

1. Demonstrate, for the class and for individuals as needed, how to begin a PowerPoint® project, inserting slide templates and filling them in.

2. Model finding pictures and inserting them into slides.

3. Allow students time to work on PowerPoint® presentations; help as needed.

4. Using the State Bibliography template transparency, demonstrate how to complete bibliography slides.

5. Have the students complete their bibliography slides using citation information from their notes.

State Research PowerPoint® Slide Lists
State Symbol
Slide 1—Title and author
Slide 2—Common and scientific name of symbol
Slide 3—Picture of symbol **and** description of symbol
Slide 4—How this became a symbol
Slide 5—Another picture **and** why this symbol was chosen to represent our state
Slide 6—Bibliography

State Person
Slide 1—Title and author
Slide 2—Birth and death dates of this person
Slide 3—Picture **and** what brought this person to our state
Slide 4—Another picture **and** description of this person
Slide 5—Contributions this person made to our state
Slide 6—Bibliography

State Place
Slide 1—Title and author
Slide 2—Where this place is located
Slide 3—Map of this place
Slide 4—Picture **and** description of this place
Slide 5—Why this place is significant to the history of our state
Slide 6—Bibliography

State Event
Slide 1—Title and author
Slide 2—Picture **and** where this event took place
Slide 3—Another picture of this event and brief caption
Slide 4—Describe this event. How did it start? Who was involved? How did it end?
Slide 5—Why this event is significant to the history of our state
Slide 6—Bibliography

Helpful Sites to Use

Netstate.com
www.netstate.com/states/index.html
This is a great resource with information about each state including symbols, places, and a little about famous people.
State animals.com
www.stateanimals.com
This has links to all the state animals and offers more in-depth descriptions of selected animals.
Infoplease—State Symbols
www.infoplease.com/ipa/A0801717.html
Includes links for every state, with highlights about history and tourist attractions, and additional links about some symbols.
First gov for kids
www.kids.gov/k_states.htm
Has links for each state that lead to more in-depth information.
The National Statuary Hall Collection
www.aoc.gov/cc/art/nsh/index.cfm
A complete list of the statutes in the Statuary Hall in Washington, D.C. Each state is represented by two people; each name is linked to a substantial biographical sketch
Travel and Tourism Web sites for U.S. States,
www.usa.gov/Citizen/Topics/Travel_Tourism/State_Tourism.shtml
Links to each state's official tourism site.

Name _____

Date _____

State Bibliography

Book

Format

First author's last name, first author's first name, second author's first name second author's last name. <u>Title</u>. Place of publication: publisher, publication date.

Example

Bledsoe, Sara. <u>Colorado</u>. Minneapolis, Minnesota: Lerner Publications, 1997.

_____

_____

_____

Website

Format

"Title if electronic document or work" [Type of medium].
Available: website/path/file. [Access date].

Example

"Denver's Characters Clara Brown" [Online]. Available: http://www.denvergov.org/AboutDenver/history_char_brown.asp [January 8, 2007].

_____

_____

_____

State Event

Write a detailed paragraph about your chosen event. Use the template below to guide you.

Name of Event

by (Your Name)

(Name of event) was important to our state history in many ways. (Name of event) (Detailed description goes here. This may take several sentences. Tell how the event began, how long it lasted, and exactly what happened.) The most notable thing about (name of event) is _____ _____.

It was important to our state history because _____.

(DON'T FORGET TO INDENT!)

_____

By _____

_____
_____
_____
_____
_____
_____
_____
_____
_____
_____
_____
_____
_____
_____
_____

State Place

Write a detailed paragraph about your chosen location. Use the template below to guide you.

Name of Place

by (Your Name)

(Name of place) was important to our state history in many ways. (Name of place) (Detailed description goes here, including location, what it looks like, etc. This may take several sentences.) Discuss how and why this place played or plays an important role in state history.

(DON'T FORGET TO INDENT!)

By _____

State Symbol

Write a detailed paragraph about your chosen symbol. Use the template below to guide you.

Name of Symbol

by (Your Name)

The (name of symbol) is a fitting symbol to our state history in many ways. The (name of symbol) (Detailed description goes here. This may take two sentences.) It represents our state because _____. The (name of symbol) became the state _____ in _____ when (something happened) _____. The (name of symbol) also known as (scientific name goes here) is a fitting symbol for our state because _____ _____.

(DON'T FORGET TO INDENT!)

_____

By _____

_____

_____

_____

_____

_____

_____

_____

_____

_____

_____

_____

_____

_____

_____

PowerPoint® Category Slide Lists:

State Symbol

Slide I-Title and author

Slide 2-Common and scientific name of symbol

Slide 3-Picture and description of symbol

Slide 4-How this became a state symbol

Slide 5-Another picture and why this symbol was chosen to represent our state

Slide 6-Bibliography

State Person

Slide 1-Title and author

Slide 2-Birth and death dates of this person

Slide 3-Picture and what brought this person to our state

Slide 4-Another picture and description of this person

Slide 5-Contributions this person made to our state

Slide 6-Bibliography

State Place

Slide 1-Title and author

Slide 2-Where this place is located

Slide 3-Map of this place

Slide 4-Picture and description of this place

Slide 5-Why this place is significant to the history of our state

Slide 6-Bibliography

State Event

Slide 1-Title and author

Slide 2-Picture and where this event took place

Slide 3-Another picture and brief caption

Slide 4-Description of this event—How did it start? Who was involved? How did it end?

Slide 5-Why this event is significant to the history of our state

Slide 6-Bibliography

The Mystery of the Bloody Beagle

• Library Lessons •

by | Sharron Cohen

Grades
4–6

To the Teacher or Librarian

Objective
To reinforce research and logical thinking skills.

Supplies
If students are using print reference resources to solve the mystery, there should be enough almanacs, atlases, dictionaries, and encyclopedias for the class to share. The atlases should have at least moderately detailed maps of individual U.S. states.

If students are using online resources to solve the mystery, there should be enough Internet-connected computers for them to share.

The following Web sites are useful for solving the mystery:

Encyclopedias and Almanacs
- Fact Monster: www.factmonster.com
- Information Please: www.infoplease.com

Dictionary
- Word Central: www.wordcentral.com

Atlas
- Mapquest: www.mapquest.com

Prepare in Advance
- Photocopy "The Mystery of the Bloody Beagle" (pages 122–123) and the Detective's Report (page 125) for each team of students.
- Show students how to use print and/or online reference resources.

How to Solve the Mystery of Research
"The Mystery of the Bloody Beagle" consists of a brief description of the crime and four suspects. Each suspect gives facts about him- or herself and the situation. Students need to decide which facts to look up and where to find them. When they check the facts, they will discover that at least one of the suspects has lied. The suspect (or suspects) who lied is guilty. Students should then use the Detective's Report to reconstruct the crime, determine who committed the crime and why, and decide where the missing item can be found.

Hint: Sometimes the actual research is easier than deciding which facts to research and where to look. It helps to have students underline the facts they want to research with a variety of colored pens. For example, they could use red for facts that require an encyclopedia, green for words that require a dictionary, purple for clues to search in an atlas, etc. That will aid their thinking process and make their research more efficient.

The Mystery of the Bloody Beagle

The Crime:

According to local legend, specters cavort in the Baneville Burying Ground on All Hallows' Eve. This year, when the sun rose on All Hallows' Day, more than the wraiths had disappeared. Sometime during the moonless night the Bloody Beagle of Baneville, a small marble monument to a revered pet, had been chiseled from its two-foot-high marble base and spirited away.

While the phantasmal visitors could not be detained for questioning, four corporeal suspects had been seen entering the graveyard during the night.

Who took the Bloody Beagle of Baneville out of the town's necropolis? Where is the Bloody Beagle hidden?

The Suspects:

Suspect 1—Rico Mortis

Rico Mortis, an antiques dealer specializing in mortuary artifacts, claims to have been born in Coffins Comer, New Jersey, which is southeast of Philadelphia, Pennsylvania, the year Robert Lawrence Stine was born.

We found Rico Mortis in his warehouse, surrounded by plastic-shrouded statues. "The Bloody Beagle is so named because of the rust-red lichens that grow on its surface," Rico Mortis informed us. "It's a nice piece of sculpture, and there has always been conjecture that it was carved by Edmonia Lewis, a young woman who was accused of attempting to poison two college classmates. Sadly, the lichens that give it its name are destroying it by producing an acid that dissolves marble. If I owned it, I would take better care of it."

Rico Mortis's Alibi: "I loathe Halloween," Rico Mortis admitted vehemently: "Some people see the night as a license to vandalize. That O'Leum punk, for instance. You don't think he was looking for trouble? I was in the cemetery that night, trying to keep the area safe from thugs and delinquents by scaring them away. If I had been there to steal the Bloody Beagle I wouldn't have called attention to myself by wearing a white sheet and wailing like a demented bloodhound."

Suspect 2—Edna Mae Ternal

Edna Mae Ternal, who calls herself Madame E. Ternal, is a practitioner of spiritualism. She claims to have been born in Casper, Wyoming, northwest of Cheyenne, the year Howard Phillips Lovecraft died.

"The Fox sisters are my spirit contacts," E. Ternal told us. "Margaret, Leah, and Catherine Fox all claimed to communicate with the dead. When they passed away in the 1890s they tried to contact the living and finally reached me. They have allowed me to bring many bereaved mourners into contact with the souls of their dearly departed, but not with my beloved Sedna. Oh, dear, I'm going to cry now. I named Sedna after an Inuit goddess. That darling, precious bulldog was my canine soul mate. She's been gone a year now, without a word from the beyond, not even the faintest little growl."

Madame E. Ternal's Alibi: "I was in my garden contemplating what kind of monument might focus Sedna's spirit enough to bring it back to me, when I heard a faint clink, clink, clinking sound from the cemetery. It was Sedna's dog tags! I recognized the sound immediately! A moment later I heard her barking! I ran into the cemetery to find her, but all I saw was that odious Combs girl who's always filming people when they aren't looking. She calls it cinema verite. I call it bad manners." E. Ternal sniffed with disapproval. "Fortunately, she had her back to me, so I had a chance to slip away undetected. Then I bumped into her cart and saw the CD player. When I realized that the barking had been a sham, I returned to my garden and collapsed in despair on Sedna's grave."

Suspect 3—*Catarina Combs*

Catarina Combs, a teenager who goes by the sobriquet Cata, is an aspiring filmmaker. She claims to have been born in Deadwood, South Dakota, south of Sioux Falls, the year that Walter de la Mare died.

"This is where I store my props," she explained, leading us into a basement workroom lined with cardboard boxes. "I have a miscellaneous collection. Over here is a replica of the cinematograph, a camera and projector invented by Louis Lumiere and his brother Alphonse. The audience was so terrified by the image of an oncoming train that they fled the theater. And here's a movie poster for Alfred Hitchcock's Psycho. It was released in 1965, way before I was born, but I hear it made women afraid to take showers. That's what I want to do. I want to make movies so scary that people will run from the theater and refuse to bathe."

Cata Comb's Alibi: "Wow! What a night! I was filming the Bloody Beagle for a scene in my new movie, Dawn of Dracula's Dogs. I was using my CD player for sound effects. Want to hear them?" Cata filled the basement workroom with a yammering cacophony before we had a chance to decline her enthusiastic offer. "And then I filmed a ghost! A real live ghost! I'm going to be famous! Look at this footage!" A few mouse-clicks on her Mac revealed a ghastly creature wailing like a banshee. We didn't have the heart to tell her it looked like Rico Mortis in a sheet.

Suspect 4—*Moss O'Leum*

Moss O'Leum claims to have been born in Tombstone, Arizona, southeast of Tucson, the year J. K. Rowling's book Harry Potter and the Philosopher's Stone was published in England.

"Go ahead, blame me," Moss O'Leum snarled belligerently. "I'm a kid. Kids always get blamed. And the Irish, too, just like my mother's favorite saint, Oliver Plunket. Even though he was an archbishop, he was hanged for crimes he didn't commit. So don't go telling me I'm going to get fair treatment from the likes of you. Or from the kids in this backwater town, either. They've been mean to me since I moved here. Paul Barer, the ringleader of all the interesting things that happen in my school, said I'd have to show up at his backyard clubhouse with a pretty spectacular gift if I wanted to join his gang."

When we pointed out that he had been seen entering the Baneville Burial Ground pulling a wagon and carrying a chisel, Moss O'Leum became even more defensive. "Ah, come on! I was dressed up like Indiana Jones! You know, Raiders of the Lost Ark, that old 1981 Steven Spielberg movie about the archaeologist who goes around stealing things from tombs. What do you expect me to carry? A bunch of bloomin' roses? And the wagon was for hauling my candy. I do a lot of trick or treating."

Moss O'Leum's Alibi: "Say, just hypothetically, that you went to the cemetery to steal the Bloody Beagle," Moss O'Leum suggested. "And say someone was weeping and someone else was wailing and dogs were barking and trees were creaking, and maybe your mother had told you all about the sounds banshees make when someone's about to die. Maybe you wouldn't hang around long enough to do what you'd intended. Not that I'm admitting anything," he added petulantly. "I'm just telling you what might have been going on in someone else's head."

Solution

Maybe there were ghosts in the Baneville Burying Ground on Halloween, and maybe there weren't, but we do know that at least four mortals were there. Each had a motive to be in an old cemetery in the dark. Rico Mortis was protecting the graveyard from potential vandals by pretending to be a ghost. Moss O'Leum intended to steal the Bloody Beagle (he had the tools and a wagon on which to cart it away), but he was too spooked to stay. Madame E. Ternal was searching for the spirit of her beloved Sedna. Because the spiritualist saw Cata Combs from the back on a moonless night, she couldn't see her clearly enough to know that, just this once, Cata Combs wasn't filming. The teenager had been chiseling the Bloody Beagle from its pedestal, using the sound effects coming from her CD player to mask the clink-clink-clink of her chisel against marble. Cata, who wanted a prop for her movie Dawn of Dracula's Dogs, is probably hiding the Bloody Beagle in a cardboard box in her basement workroom.

Information about the Suspects

Suspect 1—Rico Mortis
Coffins Corner, New Jersey, is southeast of Philadelphia, Pennsylvania.
Robert Lawrence (R. L.) Stine was born in 1943.
Sculptress Edmonia Lewis was accused of attempting to poison two classmates at Oberlin College.
Lichens, which can be red, produce acids that dissolve rock.

Suspect 2—Madame E. Ternal
Casper, Wyoming, is northwest of Cheyenne, Wyoming.
Howard Phillips (H. P.) Lovecraft died in 1937.
The Fox sisters, Margaret, Leah, and Catherine, claimed they communicated with the dead. All three died between 1890 and 1893.
Sedna was an Inuit goddess who ruled over sea animals.

Suspect 3—Cata Combs
Deadwood, South Dakota, is west, not south, of Sioux Falls, South Dakota.
Walter de la Mare died in 1956.
Louis Lumiere and his brother did invent the cinematograph, but his brother's name was Auguste, not Alphonse.
Alfred Hitchcock's movie Psycho was released in 1960, not 1965.

Suspect 4—Moss O'Leum
Tombstone, Arizona, is southeast of Tucson, Arizona.
Harry Potter and the Philosopher's Stone, by J. K. Rowling, was published in England in 1997.
Archbishop Oliver Plunket was hanged after being convicted of false charges. He was canonized (declared a saint) in 1975.
The 1981 movie Raiders of the Lost Ark was directed by Steven Spielberg.

Detective's Report

"The Mystery of the Bloody Beagle"

Suspect 1—*Rico Mortis*

Age _____   Guilty _____   Innocent _____

Facts that were researched. (Circle any that are not correct.)

Suspect 2—*Madame E. Jernal*

Age _____   Guilty _____   Innocent _____

Facts that were researched. (Circle any that are not correct.)

Suspect 3—*Cata Combs*

Age _____   Guilty _____   Innocent _____

Facts that were researched. (Circle any that are not correct.)

Suspect 4—*Moss O'Leum*

Age _____   Guilty _____   Innocent _____

Facts that were researched. (Circle any that are not correct.)

Who took the Bloody Beagle of Baneville?

Why was it taken?

Where is it hidden?

Puppets for All Purposes

• Library Lessons •

by | Pat Miller **Grades K–2, 3–5**

I was in first grade and a group of us were acting out Henny Penny. Each of us had drawn an animal and glued it to a tongue depressor. I got to be Turkey Lurkey and my traced-hand turkey was a handsome one. My teacher turned a long table on its side and we hid behind it. As our turns came to speak, we poked our puppets above the table edge and used our best animal voices. It was a transforming experience for me.

Unfortunately, I had to wait until I was a librarian to have another puppet experience and by then I was more inhibited. I wanted to introduce a unit on pet nonfiction and had a large dog puppet with legs that wrapped around my body. My idea was to have it tell dog jokes to the audience and let students feed it little dog biscuits. Feeling foolish, I opened the dog's mouth and began to speak. Immediately, as far as the children were concerned, I disappeared and they interacted with the dog. It didn't matter that I used my own voice. It didn't matter that my arm was obviously inside the body of the puppet. And it didn't matter that my cheeks were bright red. All that mattered was that I had given children an opportunity to enter the world of imagination and they willingly walked through its door.

Since then I have used many puppets. They have included a folded paper plate with a fake pearl glued inside, a small juice carton covered with quilt batting for a sheep, a gardening glove with pompom heads glued on each finger, and a finger puppet with letters that folded down into my palm as we sang BINGO.

Most ambitiously, I am the alter ego of a host puppet named Kippy Joe. He's a black bear from Folkmanis with a moveable mouth and two arms and paws that are big enough to slip my hands into. He has more outfits than I do, along with props for every season and genre. He is much more outgoing and funny than I am and delights in being mischievous. One year at Halloween, I dressed him in a sleeveless velour pumpkin costume that slipped over his head. As I introduced the books, Kippy Joe kept flashing his Power Ranger Underoos, to the delight of my students. We've celebrated his birthday and he's gotten get well cards when he was sick. He's received more than 200 postcards from students on trips. And he is very experienced at introducing topics from farm animals to poetry, Martin Luther King Jr. Day to National Humor Month Planning for Puppetry.

You don't need fancy or expensive puppets to work puppet magic. This article features five inexpensive types of puppets to make and use with lessons and read alouds, as well as patterns (see pages 130, 132–139). The supplies are easily found at your local craft or discount store and are simple enough to use with students.

As you plan for puppets, use the Puppet Planning Form on page 131. Store copies of the form with your puppets in large, zippered plastic bags. I use Microsoft® Word to keep track of my multitude of puppets and props. I record the type of puppet and which lettered box I keep it in. It's easy to locate the needed puppet using the program's search function.

Stick Puppets

Use patterns like the ones on pages 132–134 to make stick puppets from stiff felt, craft foam, cardboard, or paper plates. They can also be made from reinforced pictures cut from magazines, books, or coloring books. The sticks can be Popsicle® sticks, craft sticks, unsharpened pencils, or sturdy sticks from playground trees. You or your students can make one for each character in a story or you can have multiples of the same character so students can perform chorally.

Jan Brett provides masks of the characters from five of her books on her Web site. Go to www.jan brett.com/activities_pages_masks.htm to find patterns for The Umbrella, Gingerbread Baby, The Hat, The Mitten, and Town Mouse, Country Mouse. Print the masks and attach each to a paper plate and a craft stick handle. Do the same with the masks at www.pbskids.org/arthur/print/playmaker/masks that accompany the script for *D. W. Gets Her Library Card*.

There are more stick puppet patterns on the LibrarySparks Web site. Go to www.highsmith.com. Click on the LibrarySparks tab, then Web Resources and locate the following months at the bottom of the page:

- October 2007: Fox, Monkey, and Crocodile (*Counting Crocodiles*)
- February 2007: *Substitute Groundhog*
- November 2006: *"Buzz" Said the Bee*
- October 2006: Super Baby (*Baby Brains*)

Sock Puppets

Socks are cheap in bulk at discount stores and can also be found at dollar stores in a variety of colors. Athletic socks are durable; students can draw on them with permanent markers to make their own puppets. Features can be cut from craft foam, felt, or fabric and adhered with tacky glue (So-Fro is one brand name). Googly eyes, pompom ears, or buttons can also be glued or sewn on for features.

To make a mouth, slip the sock loosely on your hand with its heel over the knuckles at the base of your fingers. Tuck the excess length at the toe of the sock into itself in the palm of your hand, with your thumb underneath and fingers on top. Students can set up the mouth each time they use the puppet. To make a permanent mouth, pin the tucked-in fabric in place, remove your hand, and stitch it on both sides.

Paper Bag Puppets

Brown lunch sacks make serviceable puppets, but you might want to look in the gift sections of discount or craft stores. They sell better-quality bags in a rainbow of colors. You can also get white sacks from bakeries. Bag puppets are very versatile because you can draw on them and glue or staple costumes, features, and body parts to them, such as the ones on pages 135–136.

For just a few cents, each child can create and perform with his or her own puppet. For best results, leave the bag closed and slide your hand in. The tips of your fingers should slide over the creased fold in the bottom of the sack. Use the flapped part as the upper head so the puppet appears to speak.

Finger Puppets

Finger puppets can be made by adding long tabs to the sides of small patterns, and then wrapping the tabs around your fingers and taping them. See the sample patterns on page 130 or use cut-off fingers of cloth gloves. A quick and durable way to make finger puppets is to use penny or nickel coin roll wrappers. Cut them to the length you want; slip them over the fingers; and attach your picture pattern, or even a letter of the alphabet to the wrapper.

You can perform multiple-character plays with a single hand or put a puppet or two on each hand. You can even use washable markers to draw faces on the pads of each finger. This is especially convenient if you are performing a subtraction fingerplay like "Five Little Monkeys."

Overhead Puppets

Make clear or colored transparencies of characters in a book or from patterns like the ones on pages 137–139. Cut them out and use clear tape to attach them to thin bamboo skewers (sold in dollar stores and in the meat section of grocery stores) so you can manipulate them without your hands showing. Overhead puppet shows are easy for classes to view because the puppets act on a well-lit overhead stage. You can draw or duplicate simple backgrounds over which you lay your puppets.

The stage is small, so the story should have few characters and plenty of action. Overhead puppets don't require a lot of visual detail, making them a plus for artistically challenged librarians. Because characters can disappear down the bottom of the stage, this type of puppetry is good for a book like *Substitute Groundhog* in which various animals go into the groundhog's hole and pop up again.

On with the Show

Puppetry doesn't have to be a weekly thing, though your students will enjoy seeing your mascot puppet weekly. Include it every grading period and use it with all grades. Older students enjoy watching puppets as much as younger ones and will respond eagerly when invited to perform. The applause was rousing for my puppet rendition of *Anansi and the Moss-Covered Rock* whether the audience was kindergartners or fifth graders.

Puppets came in handy when I had a schedule glitch that put fifth grade and kindergarten classes together for a lesson one week. We had a lot of fun doing a paired reader's theater performance of *Bear Snores On*. Each older reader stood behind a chair in which sat a five-year-old with a puppet. When the older child read, he or she would touch the shoulder of the younger partner as a signal to make the puppet speak. It was so much fun that students asked to do it again!

Puppet Sources

If you have no budget for puppets, ask for donations from students, business partners, and through your community newspaper. Many puppets can be washed on the gentle cycle of your washing machine. List the names of business donors on a Puppet Hall of Fame on your Web page, thank them in a small ad in your yearbook, or recognize them on a nicely framed poster in your library or near the front of school. Businesses are often happy for the publicity.

- **Commercial Puppets:** Look at discount, dollar, and drug store toy aisles. Don't overlook the bath aisle, where foam bath mitts shaped like puppets are sold. I've also found puppets sold as gifts, as gloves (each finger is a puppet), and as birthday party favors.

- **Oriental Trading Company:** (www.oriental trading.com): Search the keyword "puppets" to find many puppets or puppet sets ranging from $2.99 to $29.95. They include people, animals, and props like clouds and sun for weather play. Materials include vinyl, plush, canvas, foam, and paper bags. The site sells a premium plush set of six animals that look like stuffed animals for your hand, and craft kits so kids can assemble felt, canvas, or paper bag puppets. The sets are inexpensive enough to provide a puppet for every child.

- **Folkmanis Puppets** (www.folkmanis.com): These are premier puppets for the school crowd. Folkmanis sells animals of every stripe as well as puppets that look like a small boy and girl. Most have moveable mouths and other body parts, like tails or paws. You've probably seen these gorgeous, realistic puppets on the vendor floor of major library conferences.

You don't need a fancy stage or professional puppets to put on a show your students will love to watch or perform. The major ingredients needed are enthusiasm, a spirit of fun, and maybe a little courage. Step out of your comfort zone to join children in purposeful play. They will long remember the puppetry you perform with them, even if it's just a simple traced-hand turkey and a tipped table!

Puppet Books

Note: The first six books are the ones I have relied on for years. Check www.amazon.com for those that are out of print. They are followed by more recent titles that are readily available.

Old Reliables

- *Fun Puppet Skits for Schools and Libraries* by Joanne F. Schroeder. Adventureland Press, 1995. (Call 231-864-2314 to order). Contains patterns, including one for a deluxe and durable puppet stage; scripts and the pattern to use with each of forty-five puppet plays based on folk and fairy tales, children's books, songs, and rhymes. (120 pages)

- *How to Do "The Three Bears" with Two Hands: Performing With Puppets* by Walter Minkel. American Library Association, 2000. This book supplies more of the how and why behind puppets, including developing your puppetry techniques, writing and adapting scripts, creating a puppet program, and building a puppet stage. It comes with five complete puppet show scripts. (154 pages)

- *Mitt Magic: Fingerplays for Finger Puppets* by Lynda Roberts. Gryphon House, 1985. Finger puppets or magnetic pictures in sets of five are the easiest to make and manipulate. Here are addition- and subtraction-type songs for a variety of animals and objects that fit into every kind of storytime. Includes patterns. (89 pages)

- *Leading Kids to Books through Puppets* by Caroline Feller Bauer. American Library Association, 1997. The book includes numerous scripts, stories, and rhymes to use in puppet shows, as well as lists of books that can be introduced by a puppet. (156 pages)

- *Puppets, Poems, & Songs* by Julie Catherine Shelton. Fearon Librarian Aids, 1993. Curriculum topics like Nursery Rhymes, Creepy Delights (Insects), The Briny Deep, and six others include complete instructions for making glove, paper plate, finger, and other puppets to accompany specific songs and rhymes, which are also supplied. The book begins with thirty pages of assembly techniques for nine kinds of puppets and tips for a successful presentation. (288 pages)

- *Storytelling with Puppets, Second Edition* by Connie Champlin. American Library Association, 1998. Its twenty-two chapters are divided into six units: Before the Story, The Puppets, Roles of Puppets, Participatory Storytelling, Presentation Formats (types of puppets), and After the Story. (249 pages)

More Recent Resources

- *The Complete Book of Puppetry* by George Latshaw. Dover, 2000.

- *Fee Fi Fo Fum: Puppets & Other Folktale Fun* by Linda Bair & Jill Andrews. UpstartBooks, 2005.

- *One-Person Puppetry Streamlined & Simplified: With 38 Folktale Scripts* by Yvonne Amar Frey. ALA Editions, 2005.

- *Practical Puppetry A-Z: A Guide for Librarians and Teachers* by Carol R. Exner. McFarland, 2005.

- *Puppets & Storytime: More than 100 Delightful, Skill-Building Ideas and Activities for Early Learners* by Jean R. Feldman. Scholastic, 2005.

- *A Show of Hands: Using Puppets with Young Children* by Ingrid M. Crepeau and M. Ann Richards. Redleaf Press, 2003.

- *Storytime Puppet Zoo: Simple Puppet Patterns & Plays* by Marilyn Lohnes. UpstartBooks, 2005.

Stories to Use with Puppets

- *Anansi and the Moss-Covered Rock* by Eric A. Kimmel. Holiday House, 1990.

- *Baby Brains* by Simon James. Candlewick Press, 2007.

- *Bear Snores On* by Karma Wilson. Margaret K. McElderry Books, 2003.

- *"Buzz," Said the Bee* by Wendy Cheyette Lewison. Scholastic, 2003.

- *Cork & Fuzz: Short and Tall* by Dori Chaconas. Viking, 2006.

- *Counting Crocodiles* by Judy Sierra. Harcourt, 2001.

- *Duck & Goose* by Tad Hills. Random House, 2006.

- *Good Boy, Fergus!* by David Shannon. Blue Sky Press, 2006.

- *Henny Penny* retold by Paul Galdone. Sandpiper, 1984.

- *Nutmeg and Barley: A Budding Friendship* by Janie Bynum. Candlewick Press, 2006.

- *A Splendid Friend, Indeed* by Suzanne Bloom. Boyds Mills Press, 2009.

- *Substitute Groundhog* by Pat Miller. Albert Whitman, 2006.

- *Why the Sun and the Moon Live in the Sky: An African Folktale* by Elphinstone Dayrell. Houghton Mifflin Harcourt, 1990.

Sample Finger Puppet Patterns

Puppet Planning Form

Curriculum Topic or Book Title: _____

_____

Puppets Needed: _____

_____

Class or Librarian Use: _____

_____

Props Needed: _____

_____

Prepare in Advance: _____

_____

Performance Notes: _____

_____

_____

_____

_____

_____

Stick Puppet Patterns

Stick Puppet Patterns

Stick Puppet Patterns

Paper Bag Puppets

Paper Bag Puppets

Overhead Puppet Pages

Overhead Puppet Pages

Overhead Puppet Pages

A Pair of School Stories

• Library Lessons •

by | Lynne Farrell Stover

Strange and Silly

The Fabled Fourth Graders of Aesop Elementary School by Candace Fleming and *Sideways Stories from Wayside School* by Louis Sachar have a lot in common. Both schools are populated with some "strange and silly" students and teachers. (But, as author Louis Sachar points out, most schools are!) Each book contains a series of short, fable-like stories that focus on a particular teacher, student, or silly school situation. Wayside School's teacher heroine is Mrs. Jewls, who appears in class three days after her predecessor has been turned into an apple and eaten by Louis, the yard teacher. Similarly, the students of Aesop Elementary School's fourth grade class are rescued by the larger-than-life Mr. Jupiter when no other teacher is willing to step into a classroom full of obnoxious children with a reputation for making teachers grind their teeth and become white-haired.

Even though they were published over thirty years apart, the content, character, and humor in these books illustrate that much of the goings-on in the typical elementary school classroom has remained the same. Both books make excellent class read alouds as the chapters are short, stand alone, and do not need to be read in sequence. NOTE: Students do not have to have read the featured titles to successfully participate in these library lessons.

Lesson I: The New Student

Time Required: 25–30 minutes

Introduction
School stories are populated by interesting—and often unusual—students, teachers, and support staff. Your students will have fun creating a unique "school story" character.

Objectives
- Students will use a specific writing pattern to create fictional characters.
- Students will learn about word reversals. (Words that spell a different word when reversed are referred to as semordnilaps or semi-palindromes.)

Materials
- A New Student visual (page 144)
- copies of A New Student activity sheet (page 145)
- writing and drawing tools
- optional: dice
- optional: copies of Louis Sachar books for students to check out

Procedure
1. Prepare and collect materials prior to class.
2. Introduce the lesson by displaying the visual and reading it aloud. Ask students if they know what the term is for a word, phrase, or sentence that reads the same frontward and backward. (Answer: palindrome.) Examples include radar, did, wow, and mom.

3. Explain that the words they will use for the student names in this activity are semi-palindromes or semordnilaps. "Semordnilap" ("palindrome" in reverse) is a relatively new term. A semordnilap becomes a new word when spelled in reverse. Examples include straw/warts, rats/star, and stressed/desserts. Ask students what Mrs. Drazil and Miss Nogard's names are reversed. (Answers: lizard and dragon.)

4. Distribute the activity sheets. Students may work individually or in small groups.

5. Read the directions with the students. Students may either choose the new student name on their own or use the dice.

6. Allow students to complete the journal entry and character illustration.

7. Encourage them to share their creations with the class. Anticipate interesting classroom discussions and laughter as children reveal their new students' reading interests and nicknames.

Lesson II: Exaggeration

Time Required: 20–25 minutes

Introduction
The authors of *Sideways Stories from Wayside School* and *The Fabled Fourth Graders of Aesop Elementary School* use exaggeration to make everyday events and mundane situations seem hysterically funny. Would there really be a school with a classroom on the thirtieth floor? Is it possible that a fourth grade teacher would be a Swahili-speaking, dog-grooming, hula-dancing, mummified cat-collecting, organic geochemistry-teaching, swim team-coaching, world-traveling astronaut?

Objectives
- Students will be introduced to the use of exaggeration in writing.
- Students will write exaggerated statements.

More School Stories
Students who like *The Fabled Fourth Graders of Aesop Elementary School* and *Sideways Stories from Wayside School* may also enjoy these school story picture books and novels:
- *Adam Canfield of the Slash* by Michael Winerip. Candlewick Press, 2007.
- *The Best School Year Ever* by Barbara Robinson. HarperCollins, 2005.
- *Chasing Vermeer* by Blue Balliett. Scholastic, 2005.
- *David Goes to School* by David Shannon. Blue Sky Press, 1999.
- *Dear Mr. Henshaw* by Beverly Cleary. HarperCollins, 2000.
- *Diary of a Wimpy Kid: Greg Heffley's Journal* by Jeff Kinney. Amulet Books, 2007.
- *If You Take a Mouse to School* by Laura Numeroff. HarperCollins, 2002.
- *Loser* by Jerry Spinelli. HarperCollins, 2003.
- *Lunch Money* by Andrew Clements. Atheneum, 2007.
- *No Talking* by Andrew Clements. Atheneum, 2009.
- *Sahara Special* by Esmé Raji Codell. Hyperion Books for Children, 2004.
- *The School Story* by Andrew Clements. Atheneum, 2002.
- *There's a Boy in the Girls' Bathroom* by Louis Sachar. Yearling, 1988.
- *The View from Saturday* by E. L. Konigsburg. Atheneum, 1998.

School Story Books in a Series
- *Amber Brown* by Paula Danziger
- *The Bailey School Kids* by Debbie Dadey and Marcia T. Jones
- *The Black Lagoon Adventures* by Mike Thaler
- *Cam Jansen* by David A. Adler
- *Horrible Harry* by Suzy Kline
- *Judy Moody* by Megan McDonald
- *Junie B. Jones* by Barbara Park
- *Kids of Polk Street School* by Patricia Reilly Giff
- *Magic School Bus* by Joanna Cole
- *My Weird School* by Dan Gutman
- *Shredderman* by Wendelin Van Draanen

Materials

- Exaggeration visual (see page 146)

- copies of Exaggeration activity sheet (see page 147)

- writing tools

- optional: a copy of *The Fabled Fourth Graders of Aesop Elementary School*

Procedure

1. Prepare materials ahead of class.

2. Introduce the lesson by displaying the visual. Read over the information aloud. Note: If time allows, and if a copy of *The Fabled Fourth Graders of Aesop Elementary School* is available, read pages three and four to students. (Mr. Jupiter's job interview is an excellent example of both overstatement and understatement.)

3. Distribute the activity sheets. Allow the students to work individually or in pairs.

4. Encourage students to share their examples of exaggeration with the class.

Lesson III: School Days Jeopardy

Time Required: 30–35 minutes

Natalie asked, "What's a school story?"
"A school story is just what it sounds like—it's a short novel about kids and stuff that happens mostly at school."
Natalie thought for a second and then said, "You mean like *Dear Mr. Henshaw*?"
And her mother said, "Exactly."
—*School Story* by Andrew Clements

Introduction

This quote not only defines what a school story is, it also reveals that the author, Andrew Clements, knows that school is a very important part of a child's life. That's why school stories continue to be popular. Spark students' interest in "school stuff" as they compete to see which team knows the most, or is the best at guessing!

Objectives

- Students will apply knowledge of literature and school-related themes in a competitive class activity.

- Students will apply basic addition skills to compute team scores.

Materials

- School Days Jeopardy visual or teacher-constructed game board and cards (page 148)

- School Days Jeopardy Answers (questions answer key) (page 149)

- water-soluble pen

- copies of School Days Jeopardy Score Sheet (page 150)

- writing tools

Procedure

1. Create a method for using the game cards before conducting the activity. This can be accomplished in several ways. You might make a transparency of the School Days Jeopardy game board and use sticky notes to cover the squares until students select them. Or create a game board using twenty library book pockets and poster board. Use index cards for questions and answers.

2. Introduce the activity by reading these directions to the class:

We are going to divide the class into three groups and play School Days Jeopardy. Each group will need a scorekeeper and a spokesperson. The spokesperson is responsible for conferring with team members about choosing a game card and stating the QUESTION for the answer on the card. Questions will relate to school life. For example: The question for the statement, "The author of the Wayside School stories who was once a yard teacher;" is "Who is Louis Sachar?" If a team gives an incorrect response, another team may volunteer to ask the correct question and earn the points for that card. No points will be deducted for incorrect answers. Team scorekeepers will keep a tally of points earned for all three teams. We'll compare scores at the end of the match. The team with the most points wins.

3. Organize students into groups. Have each group choose a spokesperson and scorekeeper.

4. The team with the oldest member is Team A. The team with the youngest member is Team B. The remaining team is C.

5. Start with Team A. Read the answer on the card that is picked. (If Team A gives an incorrect answer, another team may volunteer the answer and try to earn the points. However, Team B will be the next to choose from the game board. This process gives all teams equal opportunity to score.)

6. Continue play until time runs out or all game cards have been used.

7. Allow the scorekeepers to compare their tallies at the end of the game. (By having three students keeping score, a system of checks and balances is created.) If their scores are not consistent, help them come to consensus. Declare a class champion; the winning team earns "bragging rights."

Featured Titles Extension Activities

- Write an acrostic poem using the name of one of the students in either *The Fabled Fourth Graders of Aesop Elementary* or *Sideways Stories from Wayside School*. Use interesting and revealing words to describe the person. Example: Grumpy Kathy, a student at Wayside School.
  Know-it-all
  Awful
  Tattletale
  Horrible
  Yucky

- Compare the students of Wayside School to those of Aesop Elementary. How are they alike? How are they different?

- What do you think Wayside School or Aesop Elementary School looks like? Draw a picture of the classroom, library, cafeteria, or the front of the school; your choice.

- Write a "school story" fable. A fable is a short narrative that illustrates a lesson, or moral. (The ancient Greek slave, Aesop, is recognized as the most prolific fable teller. Over six hundred fables are attributed to him.) Create your own moral or use one on the list below:
  - A hero is brave in deeds as well as words.
  - Beauty is only skin-deep.
  - The best intentions will not always ensure success.
  - Birds of a feather flock together.
  - Evil wishes, like chickens, come home to roost.
  - Fine feathers don't make fine birds.
  - Look before you leap.

  - Might makes right.
  - Pride goes before destruction.
  - Self help is the best help.
  - Union is strength.

- One word can have many meanings. For example, Louis Sachar uses the word STORY, in *Sideways Stories from Wayside School*, to mean both a "fictional tale" and the "horizontal division of a building." So it's possible to have thirty stories from the thirty stories of Wayside School! The words on the list below have multiple meanings. Try to use two or more meanings of each word in a single sentence.
  - bark
  - bat
  - trip
  - toast
  - train
  - rose
  - roll
  - spring
  - place
  - light
  - fool
  - check
  - bank

- Investigate fable books in your library. Check out and read one that interests you. Fables are a type of folklore. They are shelved in the 398s in the Dewey Decimal system.

- Dramatize one of Aesop's fables or a fable written in class. Interrupt the action before the ending that reveals the lesson learned. Encourage the audience to guess the fable's moral.

- Have students imagine that they are in either Mrs. Jewls's or Mr. Jupiter's class and write stories about their experiences. Collect the stories and combine them in a class book with a funny title that reflects the personality of the class and includes the name of the school.

A New Student

In *Sideways Stories from Wayside School*, the students start off the year with Mrs. Gorf, who is soon replaced by Mrs. Jewls. Reverse the spelling of GORF and it is FROG. (Mrs. Drazil and Miss Nogard show up as substitute teachers in *Wayside School Gets a Little Stranger*. What are their names reversed?)

What if a new student showed up and, like Mrs. Gorf, had a first and last name that spelled a new word when reversed? What if these names revealed something about this person's personality?

The journal entry below makes some predictions about Pam May, a new student, based on the reversed reading of her name.

Journal Entry

A new student joined our class today.
Her name is PAM MAY.

I bet one of her favorite things to do is to study geography because her first name written backwards spells MAP.

Pam will likely check out an ATLAS when our class visits the library.

I think a good nickname for Pam would be "sweet potato" because her last name written backwards spells YAM.

A New Student

Directions: Pretend a new student has enrolled in Wayside School, and, like Mrs. Gorf, this person's name spells out a word when written back-to-front.

GORF = FROG

Use the grid below to select a first and last name for the new student. Fill out the missing information in the journal entry. Then make a drawing of the new student. Be prepared to share your work with the class.

Name Grid

First Name	Last Name
1. Pat	1. Flog
2. Star	2. Gnik
3. Ned	3. Pots
4. Ward	4. Loots
5. Leon	5. Straw
6. Meg	6. Dear

Sketch of New Student

Journal Entry

A new student joined our class today.

_____ name is _____.
(His/Her)   (first and last names selected from Name Grid)

I bet one of _____ favorite things to do is to _____
                    (his/her)   (an activity related to name)

because _____ first name written backwards spells _____.
              (his/her)   (reversed spelling of first name)

_____ will likely check out a/an _____when our class visits the library.
(student's name)   (type of book related to name)

I think a good nickname for _____ would be "_____" because
                              (student's name)   (funny nickname)

_____ last name written backwards spells _____.
(his/her)   (reversed spelling of last name)

Exaggeration

When an author exaggerates, he usually starts with factual information. Then he adds something absurdly overstated to make the characters and situations astonishing and funny. Often, the humor comes from pictures and the exaggeration created in readers' minds.

An example of exaggeration from *The Fabled Fourth Graders of Aesop Elementary School* is:

Factual Statement:
Aesop Elementary School had many items in its lost and found box.

Exaggeration:
"The place looked magical—almost like Aladdin's cave. Instead of heaps of gold and mountains of jewels, however, there were heaps of snow boots and mountains of bean bag animals."

An example of exaggeration from *Sideways Stories from Wayside School* is:

Factual Statement
Dana, a student at Wayside School, had beautiful eyes.

Exaggeration:
"And if she had a hundred eyes, all over her face and her arms and her feet, why, she would have been the most beautiful creature in the world."

Exaggeration

Directions: Write an example of exaggeration for each factual statement. Be prepared to share your work with the class.

1 The book was funny.

_____

_____

2 Paige Turner liked being a librarian.

_____

_____

3 Jupiter enjoyed reading to his students.

_____

_____

4 Gorf was a mean teacher.

_____

_____

5 Myron was a good class president.

_____

_____

School Days Jeopardy

Name that Genre	Authors who Once Were Teachers	And the Subject Is . . .	Rhyme Time
10 a short tale that teaches a lesson or moral (examples: *The Tortoise and the Hare*, *The Fox and the Grapes*)	**10** She wrote the Harry Potter Series.	**10** 2+2=4 22–3=19 6x4=24	**10** a library burglar
20 an imaginary tale containing magic and fantasy creatures (examples: *Hansel and Gretel* and *Beauty and the Beast*)	**20** He is known for his Alice in Wonderland books.	**20** basketball jump rope running	**20** a law in a place where students are taught
30 A story that explains the customs and beliefs of a people (examples: *Jason and the Argonauts* and *Demeter and Persephone*)	**30** She is the author of the Little House on the Prairie series.	**30** atlases capitals regions	**30** atlas ambush
40 A humorous story that uses outrageous exaggeration (examples: Paul Bunyan stories and Pecos Bill stories)	**40** He wrote the *Chronicles of Narnia*.	**40** painting sculpting drawing	**40** broad piece of playground equipment
50 A brief work of fiction that focuses on a single event (examples: "The Gift of Magi" and "The Monkey's Paw")	**50** His school stories include *Frindle*, *The Janitor's Boy*, *Lunch Money*, and *The Landry News*.	**50** singing instruments scales	**50** arithmetic trail

School Days Jeopardy Answers

Name that Genre	Authors who once Were Teachers	And the Subject Is ...	Rhyme Time
10 What is a ... Fable?	**10** Who is ... J. K. Rowling?	**10** What is ... Math?	**10** What is a ... Book Crook?
20 What is a ... Fairy Tale?	**20** Who is ... Lewis Carroll?	**20** What is ... Physical Education?	**20** What is a ... School Rule?
30 What is a ... Myth?	**30** Who is ... Laura Ingalls Wilder?	**30** What is ... Geography?	**30** What is a ... Map Trap?
40 What is a ... Tall Tale (or Folktale)	**40** Who is ... C. S. Lewis?	**40** What is ... Art?	**40** What is a ... Wide Slide?
50 What is a ... Short Story?	**50** Who is ... Andrew Clements?	**50** What is ... Music?	**50** What is a ... Math Path?

School Days Jeopardy

Score Sheet

TEAM A		TEAM B		TEAM C	
1.	_____	1.	_____	1.	_____
2.	_____	2.	_____	2.	_____
total	_____	total	_____	total	_____
3.	_____	3.	_____	3.	_____
total	_____	total	_____	total	_____
4.	_____	4.	_____	4.	_____
total	_____	total	_____	total	_____
5.	_____	5.	_____	5.	_____
total	_____	total	_____	total	_____
6.	_____	6.	_____	6.	_____
total	_____	total	_____	total	_____
7.	_____	7.	_____	7.	_____
total	_____	total	_____	total	_____
8.	_____	8.	_____	8.	_____
total	_____	total	_____	total	_____
9.	_____	9.	_____	9.	_____
total	_____	total	_____	total	_____
10.	_____	10.	_____	10.	_____
total	_____	total	_____	total	_____
11.	_____	11.	_____	11.	_____
total	_____	total	_____	total	_____
12.	_____	12.	_____	12.	_____
total	_____	total	_____	total	_____
13.	_____	13.	_____	13.	_____
total	_____	total	_____	total	_____
14.	_____	14.	_____	14.	_____
total	_____	total	_____	total	_____
15.	_____	15.	_____	15.	_____
total	_____	total	_____	total	_____
Grand Total _____		**Grand Total** _____		**Grand Total** _____	

Playing in the Library

• Library Lessons •

by | Pat Miller   **Grades K–2, 3–5**

The game was Library Four Corners with partners that paired a fourth grader and a kindergartner. After the second game, a winded and smiling five-year-old threw his arms around my legs and said, "I love the library! Can we play every day?"

You won't be able to play every day, but you can shatter the stereotype of the library as a stodgy, quiet place by occasionally playing learning games with your students. The pleasure and fun of the lesson will help students appreciate the library as a place that's relevant to them. Research shows that attaching an emotion to an event, whether positive or negative, helps one to remember it. Children are more likely to remember the parts of a book or the six steps in problem solving if they play games to learn them because the pleasurable emotions help lock in the learning.

Action Games

Parts of the Library

A good game to get students acquainted with the main parts of the library is Library Four Corners. Designate four areas of the library—Fiction, Everybody, Nonfiction, and Reference—with carpet squares. Reproduce and cut out the game cards on page 156 and put them in an envelope. Name the areas for students and explain the game. Have all students choose an area and stand on or near that carpet square. When you say "go," students have about twenty seconds to move from the corner they are in to another corner of their choice. They can also stay put. When the time is up, say "stop." Students must be in a corner. Draw a card and read it. Students in the corresponding section are out, and sit down in a pre-designated area of the library. Remaining students choose another corner. Continue until one child remains.

If time allows, play again, letting the child who was left be the caller. To keep the game from becoming too rowdy, tell students they will be disqualified if they make any noise, and they must sit immediately when they're out. Praise them at intervals for traveling quietly. This game is a favorite and can be played any time you need to get the wiggles, giggles, or inertia out of your students.

Types of Books

Play the next game with students seated in chairs facing each other in a circle. Give each child a book, making sure that nonfiction, biography, chapter fiction, and picture books (both fiction and nonfiction) are represented. For older students, play in a similar manner with a variety of literary genres. Ask students to look over their book and determine if it is fiction or nonfiction and if it is suitable for beginning or experienced readers. Then play Stand Up, Sit Down. Each time you make a statement, students who have a book that matches will stand. If they are correct, they can sit down in their chair. If incorrect, they are out and must sit on the floor. The game proceeds until you run out of statements. Those remaining can check out an extra book. You can have students exchange books to play a second round. Repeating the game motivates students to quickly learn about book types.

Stand Up, Sit Down Statements

My book could never happen in real life.
My book has chapters.
My book has colored illustrations.
My book is a biography.
My book is best for beginning readers.
My book is fiction.
My book is full of facts.
My book is nonfiction.
My book was written from imagination.
My book is best for experienced readers.

Literary Games

White House Pets Jeopardy

Serve up a little history with your library play, using Gibbs Davis's book *Wackiest White House Pets* (Scholastic, 2004). Feature books on pets or presidents, along with animal puppets or stuffed animals, in a display. Read the book aloud, in a single session or in sections over several classes. Then play Wacky White House Pets Jeopardy by having student teams answer the questions on pages 157–158. Make the board (page 159) and the question sheets into transparencies so students can read the choices with you. Use paper with an appropriately sized window cut from it to mask the rest of the questions. Place an "x" across each square of the Jeopardy grid after it's been chosen. Teams earn the number of points in the square if they answer correctly. An incorrect answer subtracts that number from their team score. All questions and answers come from Davis's book.

The answers are:

Gift Pets: b, c, d, d
Talented Pets: a, a, d, c
Useful Pets: d, b, d, a
Exotic Pets: a, d, c, b

Other suggested books:

- *Animals in the House: A History of Pets and People* by Sheila Keenan. Scholastic Nonfiction, 2007.

- *If the Walls Could Talk: Family Life at the White House* by Jane O'Connor. Simon & Schuster, 2004.

- *Pets at the White House* by Marge Kennedy. Children's Press, 2009.

- *President Adams' Alligator and Other White House Pets* by Peter Barnes. VSP Books, 2003.

Paper, Scissors, Rock

After you read a story set in China or as part of a Chinese New Year Celebration, teach students to play Jen-dow, Shih-toe, Boo (Scissors, Paper, Rock). Give student pairs a copy of the game visual on page 155. Chant the three words as partners raise their fists up and down to the chant. On "Boo," students show their choice of the three. Five fingers stretched out are Jen-dow; two form Shih-toe; a clenched fist is Boo. Jen-dow cuts Shih-toe, Shih-toe covers Boo, and Boo breaks Jen-dow. Keep score if desired, using five kidney beans or buttons in a cup. Each time a player wins, that player takes a bean or button from his or her cup and one from the other player. The first player to earn all five counters is the champion.

Suggested books are:

- *Cat and Rat: The Legend of the Chinese Zodiac* by Ed Young. Henry Holt & Company, 1998.

- *The Empty Pot* by Demi. Henry Holt & Company, 2007.

- *The Magical Monkey King: Mischief in Heaven: Classic Chinese Tales* retold by Ji-Li Jiang. Shen's Books, 2004.

Mother, May I?

Before reading a story with Spanish words in it, play ¿Mama, Puedo? (pronounced pway-doh), a version of Mother May I? Enlarge and make a copy or transparency of the translations on page 153, and display it for student reference. Line students up along a starting line in groups of three. The trios move together. Choose a caller (you may want to start to show students how it is done). Play like the traditional game, except students will move in ways the animal would. Have students demonstrate how they would move for each animal before you begin the play.

¿Mamá, puedo?

Numbers

uno = 1

dos = 2

tres = 3

quatro = 4

cinco = 5

Animals

el caballo = horse

el cerdo = pig

el perro = dog

la culebra = snake

la hormiga = ant

el gallo = rooster

Follow with one of these student favorites:

- *The Bossy Gallito = El Gallo de Bodas: A Traditional Cuban Folktale* retold by Lucia M. Gonzalez. Scholastic, 1999.

- *Oh No, Gotta Go!* by Susan Middleton Elya. Penguin Putnam, 2003.

- *Tortuga in Trouble* by Ann Whitford Paul. Holiday House, 2009.

Books of Library Games

There are many books that give directions for games. You can adapt ideas for classroom games to suit library objectives, or use the following titles that are designed specifically for libraries.

Battle of the Books and More: Reading Activities for Middle School Students by Sybilla Cook, Frances Corcoran, and Beverley Fonnesbeck. Alleyside Press, 2001. Includes instructions for the battle and questions for 250 popular and classic titles read by grades four and up. See also *Elementary Battle of the Books* (UpstartBooks, 2005) for grades K–5.

Dewey and the Decimals: Learning Games & Activities by Paige Taylor and Kent & Susan Brinkmeyer. Alleyside Press, 2001. The authors developed a number of games for teaching the Dewey Decimal system, as well as for call numbers, book location, and online catalogs.

57 Games to Play in the Library or Classroom by Carol K. Lee and Fay Edwards. UpstartBooks, 1997. Most of these are board games designed for play by the whole class. Instructions, patterns, and sample questions are included for games suitable to a variety of grades.

Fun-brarian: Games, Activities, & Ideas to Liven up Your Library! by Kathleen Fox. UpstartBooks, 2007. Twenty quick, simple games plus a handful of clever ideas and reproducibles add zip to your efforts to introduce or reinforce basic library skills, book care, sharing favorite titles, and more.

Learning About Books & Libraries: A Gold Mine of Games by Carol K. Lee and Janet Langford. UpstartBooks, 2000. Find instructions here for forty-seven games. They are divided into games using fiction books to review medal winners, authors, and fiction features; games to reinforce location and reference skills; and games based on popular children's books or thematic units.

Library Mania: Games & Activities for Your Library by Charlene C. Cali. UpstartBooks, 2009. In this well-designed book, Cali offers fifty library lessons that incorporate fun exercises, worksheets, and games to add zip and interest to library learning. Games, songs, reproducibles, and book lists address everything from literary genres to call numbers and parts of a book to research skills.

Ready-to-Use Library Skills Games: Reproducible Activities for Building Location and Literature Skills by Ruth Snoddon. Center for Applied Research in Education, 1987. Teach students to use the parts of libraries and books, reference materials, the Dewey Decimal system, and much more. Patterns, sample questions, instructions, grade levels, and an index make this a useful source as you prepare for next week's lessons.

The Reference Information Skills Game by Myram Forney Tunnicliff and Susan Sheldon Soenen. Libraries Unlimited, 1995. The game is based on one aspect of information skills-fact location. A question is posted on a bulletin board each day with a catchy clue. (What uses its eyes to help it swallow?) Each day an additional clue is posted until students can guess the answer. They must also supply the "search map" or reference steps they used to find the answer (form provided). There are 162 questions with clues grouped by animals, plants, and people so the game is ready to use.

Ready-Made Games for Library Skills

Adapt commercial games to library needs by changing the cards, making the moves along a board game correspond to questions on a duplicated sheet, or by having students name a fiction or nonfiction book before they can jump a checker, move along the Chutes and Ladders, or lay down a matching pair of playing cards. If your budget allows you to save work and time, purchase these games at www.highsmith. com.

Book Look is a game in which students in grades three through five match fiction and nonfiction books to their corresponding spine label cards.

Dewey® Match? is for students in grades one through three. They use twenty-five pairs (pictures and numbers) to match a classification number with its subject. Play using Memory, Go Fish, or Snap rules. For a versatile card game that can be played like a combination of password and charades, play *Media Motion.* Fourth through sixth graders try to name library terms based on their classmates' clues. To teach book location in a fun manner, use *Shelf Finder.* Then send them on a library scavenger hunt using the cards from *The Book Hunt.*

If your students are like mine, they have trouble finding books because they don't know how to alphabetize author names. Use the *Sticks and Stones* game to help all grades learn. The game includes cardboard alphabet stones and author sticks. Students match them up. Three different levels of matching help students alphabetize to the first letter, second letter, and third letter.

For a fast-paced research game, send students on *The Ultimate Expedition.* The game includes 100 challenge cards that have student teams in grades four through six racing against one another to complete research that will help them cross the globe to return to their starting point.

Playing library learning games is noisy, fun, and a great way to help students remember what you are teaching them. Don't be surprised to find you enjoy them as much as the students!

Jen–dow, Shih–toe, and Boo

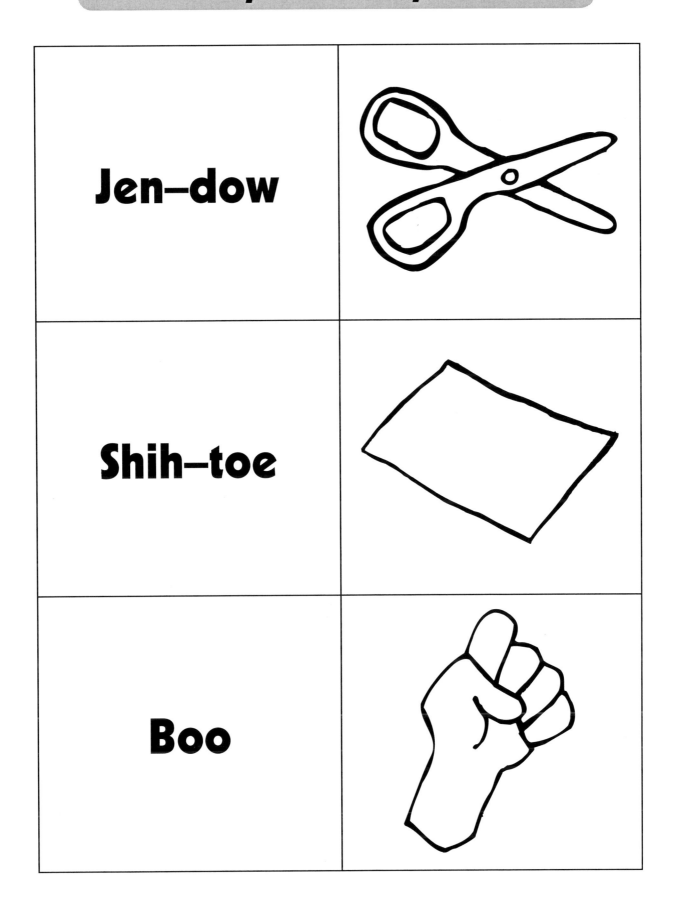

Jen–dow

Shih–toe

Boo

Library Four Corners

Fiction	Nonfiction	Everybody	Reference
Fiction	Nonfiction	Everybody	Reference
Fiction	Nonfiction	Everybody	Reference
Fiction	Nonfiction	Everybody	Reference
Fiction	Nonfiction	Everybody	Reference
Fiction	Nonfiction	Everybody	Reference

White House Pets Jeopardy Questions

Gift Pets

The king of Spain gave President George Washington a
a. parrot
b. jackass
c. guinea pig
d. shark

President Thomas Jefferson's pet grizzly bear cubs were gifts from
a. the king of France
b. his wife Dolley
c. Meriwether Lewis and William Clark
d. a pet store

President Ronald Reagan got his pet goldfish
a. from the Japanese ambassador
b. when he rescued the fish from a pond
c. from a woman who was a fan of his movies
d. in the mail from a ten-year-old boy

President Kennedy's little white dog named Pushinka
a. was a gift from his rival, Soviet Premier Nikita Khrushchev
b. was examined for "bugs" as a possible spy
c. had "pupniks" with the Kennedy's Welsh terrier, Charlie
d. all of the above

Talented Pets

Which talented White House pet could play the National Anthem on a toy trumpet?
a. Kennedy's rabbit, Zsa Zsa
b. Teddy Roosevelt's one-legged rooster
c. Andrew Johnson's secret pet mouse
d. Calvin Coolidge's raccoon, Rebecca

Which First Lady had a talking parrot that helped her entertain at White House parties?
a. Dolley Madison
b. Mrs. Calvin Coolidge
c. Barbara Bush
d. Nancy Reagan

Thomas Jefferson had a pet who sang duets with its presidential owner. "Dicky" was
a. a parrot
b. a hound dog
c. a zebra
d. a mockingbird

Millie, a springer spaniel remembered for her White House doggy autobiography, belonged to
a. President Franklin Roosevelt
b. President and Mrs. Bill Clinton
c. President and Mrs. George Herbert Walker Bush
d. First Lady Jackie Kennedy

Useful Pets

President Woodrow Wilson's sheep performed which service at the White House?
a. gave wool for all the president's sweaters
b. provided milk for the first family's breakfast
c. woke up the president with their bleating
d. kept the White House lawn cut

First Lady Louisa Adams had which useful pets?
a. egg-producing hens
b. spinning silkworms
c. alarm-clock roosters
d. watchdog German shepherds

President William Taft's favorite milk-producing cow was named
a. Bessie
b. Mooly Wooly
c. Bow Wow Cow
d. Pauline Wayne

Which president used horses for transportation?
a. George Washington
b. George H. W. Bush
c. John F. Kennedy
d. Calvin Coolidge

Exotic Pets

Emily Spinach was

a. President Teddy Roosevelt's daughter's snake
b. President Abraham Lincoln's son Tad's goat
c. First Lady Dolley Madison's green parrot
d. President Franklin Pierce's "sleeve dog"

President James Buchanan's elephants were

a. symbols of the Republican Party
b. gifts from the king of Siam
c. sent to live at the local zoo
d. all of the above

The alligator at the White House during John Quincy Adams's presidency wasn't really the President's pet. Instead, it was

a. an intruder from the Potomac River that wouldn't stay away
b. on loan from a traveling circus
c. visiting with the French Marquis de Lafayette
d. his son's constant companion

Which of these was NOT among the menagerie of animals owned by the first family during Theodore Roosevelt's presidency?

a. a lion
b. a gorilla
c. a zebra
d. a hyena

White House Pets Jeopardy Game Board

Gift Pets	Talented Pets	Useful Pets	Exotic Pets
10	10	10	10
20	20	20	20
30	30	30	30
40	40	40	40
50	50	50	50

Westward Ho!

• Library Lessons

by | Lynne Farrell Stover Grades 3–6

During the nineteenth century, hundreds of thousands of freedom-loving people made the decision to pack up their families and possessions and head for the American West. They did not care that Oregon and California weren't yet states, or that accurate maps of the western territory did not exist. The life these brave pioneers pursued was filled with the possibility of a prosperous future and the guarantee of unknown hardships.

You Wouldn't Want to Be an American Pioneer! A Wilderness You'd Rather Not Tame by Jacqueline Morley is a book that focuses on these hardships. Humorously illustrated and just thirty-two pages long, it manages to contain most of the components of a good nonfiction reference book: a table of contents, an introduction, a glossary, and an index. A good companion book is *Daily Life in a Covered Wagon* by Paul Erickson (Penguin, 1997). Also well illustrated and full of fun information, this forty-eight-page book features fictional journal entries, glossary, index, and a list of relevant places to visit.

Note: It is not necessary for the students to have read the featured titles to successfully participate in the following library lessons. Extension activities can be found on page 164.

Lesson I: Westward Ho! A Dramatic Story

Time Required: 15–20 minutes

Introduction
Between 1840 and 1870 more than a quarter million pioneers traveled the 2,000 mile long Oregon Trail. Motivated by prospects of abundant resources and the possibility of free land, they were willing to spend six months of hardship and danger to start a new life.

Objectives
Students will participate in an interactive, teacher narrated, dramatic story based on life on a wagon train while traveling the Oregon Trail.

Materials
- Copies of Westward, Ho! script (see page 165)
- *(optional)* Various nonfiction books based on American pioneers, frontier life, and nineteenth-century American history

Procedure
1. Prepare the script ahead of time.
2. Introduce students to the story by explaining that this dramatic reading activity is based on one day in the life of a pioneer boy travelling with a wagon train on the Oregon Trail. Explain

that it will take the whole class to make drama successful.

3. Distribute scripts to students.

4. Assign roles. In a small group all may participate; in a large class half could take the even numbers and the other half the odd numbers.

5. Read Westward, Ho! aloud, pausing at the bold-print words to prompt student response. If time allows, read the script twice. Make the first reading the rehearsal, and the second the main event.

6. Encourage students to write their own dramatic plays.

Lesson 2: Westward Wagon Research

Time Required: 35–45 minutes

Introduction

America has always been home to pioneers—adventurous men and women willing to challenge boundaries of knowledge or travel to unfamiliar places looking for better opportunities. Some pioneers to the American West may not have been eager to join wagon trains if they had first researched where they were going and how difficult it would be to get there. Dust off the library's encyclopedias and give students an opportunity to do some exploring of their own as they participate in a fun and fast-paced research activity.

Objectives

• Students will use encyclopedias to research specific topics.

• Students will review the definitions of fact and opinion.

• Students will list three facts and two opinions related to their research topics.

Materials

• Westward Wagon Research (Fact & Opinion/Topic List) Visual 1 on page 166.

• Westward Wagon Research Sample Visual 2 on page 167.

• Westward Wagon Research activity sheet on page 168.

• encyclopedias

• writing tools

• markers, colored pencils, or crayons

• (optional) scissors

Procedure

1. Prepare materials prior to class.

2. Introduce this research lesson based on the American pioneers as they traveled west to settle unclaimed land. The reference tools used will be "old-fashioned" hard-copy encyclopedias. Explain that encyclopedias are sets of books, organized alphabetically, containing information on many subjects.

3. Display Visual 1 and read it aloud.

4. Allow the students to choose one of the topics listed. You might supply index cards for students to write down their choices.

5. Display Visual 2 as a sample. Review contents with the students.

6. Distribute the Westward Wagon Research activity sheet. Students may work independently or in small groups.

7. Show students where the encyclopedias are located and help them select the volumes they need to complete the exercise. For example, you may need to remind students that information on Davy Crocket is found in the C Volume.

8. At the end of the session, invite students to share interesting facts they discovered.

9. If time allows, create a class wagon train by cutting out the activity sheets and displaying them on a bulletin board or wall.

Lesson 3: Famous Frontier Folks—Fact or Fiction?

Time Required: 20–25 minutes

Introduction
Pioneers were strong, brave, and resourceful. Some stood out as being exceptional. Were these exceptional characters real or the product of storytellers' imaginations?

Objectives
- Students will participate in an activity identifying historical and literary figures.
- Students will complete a worksheet concerning fact and fiction.

Materials
- Famous Frontier Folks—Fact or Fiction? visual (see page 169)
- Famous Frontier Folks—Fact or Fiction? activity sheet and answer key (see pages 170–171)
- pens and/or pencils

Procedure
1. Prepare materials prior to class.

2. Start by asking students to tell you the difference between fact and fiction. (A fact is something that can be verified to be true; fiction is something created from someone's imagination.)

3. Display the Famous Frontier Folks—Fact or Fiction? visual. Read the introduction aloud. Solicit answers for the characters listed.

- Billy the Kid: Fact (aka William H. Bonney, a 19th-century outlaw)

- Caddie Woodlawn: Fiction (main character in a book by Carol Ryrie Brink)

- Calamity Jane: Fact (Martha Jane Canary, a Montana tomboy who rode for the Pony Express)

- Febold Feboldson: Fiction (a Nebraska folk hero who fought droughts)

4. Distribute the Famous Frontier Folks—Fact or Fiction? activity sheet. Students may work independently or in groups. Or use the activity sheet as a visual and complete the activity as a teacher-directed interactive lesson.

5. Read the directions to the class. Allow about ten minutes to complete the assignment.

6. Check answers as a group.

Additional Resources

Nonfiction Series

Students who enjoy reading about history from a "weird and funny" perspective may enjoy these nonfiction series:

- **Don't Know Much About . . .**
  Sample title: *Don't Know Much About the Pioneers* by Kenneth Davis. HarperCollins, 2003.

- **How Would You Survive**
  Sample title: *How Would You Survive in the American West?* by Jacqueline Morley. Children's Press, 1997.

- **If You . . .**
  Sample title: *If You Traveled West in a Covered Wagon* by Ellen Levine. Scholastic, 1992.

- **You Wouldn't Want to . . .**
  Sample title: *You Wouldn't Want to Live in a Wild West Town! Dust You'd Rather Not Settle* by Peter Hicks. Franklin Watts, 2002.

Fiction

Students who find frontier life fascinating may be interested in these fiction titles:

- *Buffalo Before Breakfast* by Mary Pope Osborne. Random House, 1999.

- *Caddie Woodlawn* by Carol Ryrie Brink. Simon & Schuster Books for Young Readers, 1997.

- *Dear Levi: Letters from the Overland Trail* by Elvira Woodruff. Yearling, 2000.

- *Francis Tucket* series by Gary Paulsen. Random House Children's Books

- *Little House* series by Laura Ingalls Wilder. HarperCollins.

- *Night of the Full Moon* by Gloria Whelan. Random House Children's Books, 2006.

- *Westward to Home: Joshua's Oregon Trail Diary* by Patricia Hermes. Scholastic, 2002.

Westward Ho!

Extension Activities

Invite students to:

1. Write a humorous story about pioneers traveling west from an unusual perspective. What might the covered wagon, a pair of shoes, or a team of mules think about such a long and dangerous journey?

2. Put together a diorama of a wagon train in action. For example: crossing a river, trading at a frontier fort, struggling through a storm, or making camp on the prairie.

3. Design a travel brochure that showcases all of the wonderful and not-so-wonderful things a person would find after they left their home and traveled to Oregon on a wagon train.

4. Make a game board that depicts a wagon train traveling the Oregon Trail as it struggles to cross the prairie to settle on a homestead on the West Coast.

5. Create a "Pioneer Cookbook" by collecting recipes that contain the main food items carried on a covered wagon such as beans, cornmeal, flour, dried apples, bacon, coffee, and sugar.

6. Conduct a debate or panel discussion addressing the costs and benefits of leaving your home and traveling to an unknown location.

7. Pretend to be a pioneer and write a letter to a relative back home who is considering joining the next wagon train traveling west. The letter should include three positive things about your experiences as well as three negative things.

8. Create a pioneer trivia game. Topics could include dangerous animals, covered wagon cooking, frontier forts, weird weather, pioneer people, and types of transportation.

9. Research the construction of the covered wagons used by the pioneers and build a model of one.

10. Draw a picture of a "well dressed" pioneer, labeling all of his or her important accessories.

Westward, Ho!

A Day on the Oregon Trail
A Dramatic Story

1. Rifle ("bang-bang")
2. Covered Wagon (wave arms in the air)
3. Pioneers ("Westward Ho!")
4. Johnnycakes ("yum-yum")
5. Buffalo (Stomp feet)
6. Rattlesnake ("hissss")
7. Tornado (stand up and turn around)

The sun was not yet up when a shot from a **rifle** startled Wade Waters from his deep sleep. He sat up quickly and bumped his head on the **covered wagon** sheltering him. It was going to be another hot day on the Oregon Trail and he and the other **pioneers** needed to get the **covered wagons** ready to travel another ten miles of their 2,000-mile trip.

Wade was not looking forward to this day's journey. It was his turn to walk beside the **covered wagon** while his older sister got to ride inside. After eating a plate of **johnnycakes** and hitching up the oxen to the **covered wagon,** the wagon train started out.

As Wade trudged along with the other **pioneers** he saw a large dust cloud in the distance. He began to worry. What if this was a **buffalo** stampede? A large herd of **buffalo** could destroy a wagon train. Maybe it was a Native American hunting party. If so, he hoped they were a friendly tribe that would trade fresh meat for some things that the **pioneers** had brought along to barter with. Wade was so worried about the dust cloud that he almost stepped on a **rattlesnake**!

He ran beside the **covered wagon** and pointed the dust cloud out to his father. His father said it looked like a **tornado**! As they looked on, the **tornado** changed direction and moved away. This was a great relief. Wade was glad it had not been a **buffalo** stampede. He was also relieved he had missed the **rattlesnake**. An encounter with a **tornado** would have been awful, too!

The day would soon be over. The **pioneers** would stop and unload their **covered wagons**, eat **johnnycakes** for supper, and then go hunting with their **rifles**. Tomorrow Wade would continue his journey on the Oregon Trail.

Westward Wagon Research

Lesson II - Visual 1

Fact – Anything that can be checked out or verified to be true.
A factual statement can be proven true with research by using books, the Internet, interviews, and observation.

Opinion – A statement that tells a person's viewpoint or belief.
An opinion cannot be proven true or false. However, it can be supported by facts.

Example:

Opinion

The covered wagons the pioneers traveled in were cramped and uncomfortable.

Facts Supporting This Opinion

- Wagons would be filled with all the supplies necessary for the long trip.
- Wagons were made of wood.
- They were usually twelve feet long, four feet wide, and two feet deep.
- The canvas "bonnet" was five feet above the wagon bed.
- The only set of springs was under the driver's seat.
- Sometimes the heat of the prairie would cause the wood of the wagon wheels to shrink and their iron rims would roll off.

Westward Wagon Research Topics

1. Boonesborough
2. Daniel Boone
3. Jim Bridger
4. Buffalo (Bison)
5. Kit Carson
6. Covered Wagon
7. Davy Crocket
8. Wyatt Earp
9. Fort Laramie
10. John Freemont
11. Geronimo
12. Wild Bill Hickok
13. Johnny Appleseed
14. Annie Oakley
15. Oregon Trail
16. Paul Bunyan
17. Pecos Bill
18. Quilt
19. Rattlesnake
20. Sitting Bull
21. Sutter's Mill
22. Tornado
23. Wagon Train
24. Laura Ingalls Wilder
25. Brigham Young
Student Choice (*with permission*)

Topic: American Buffalo

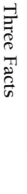

Three Facts
1. The American buffalo is a bovine mammal and is actually a bison.
2. This animal can be six feet tall and weigh between 900-2000 pounds.
3. In the nineteenth century the buffalo was almost hunted to extinction.

Opinion #1
Buffalo are
funny-looking.

Opinion #2
A buffalo would
make a bad pet

Westward Wagon Research

Lesson II - Activity

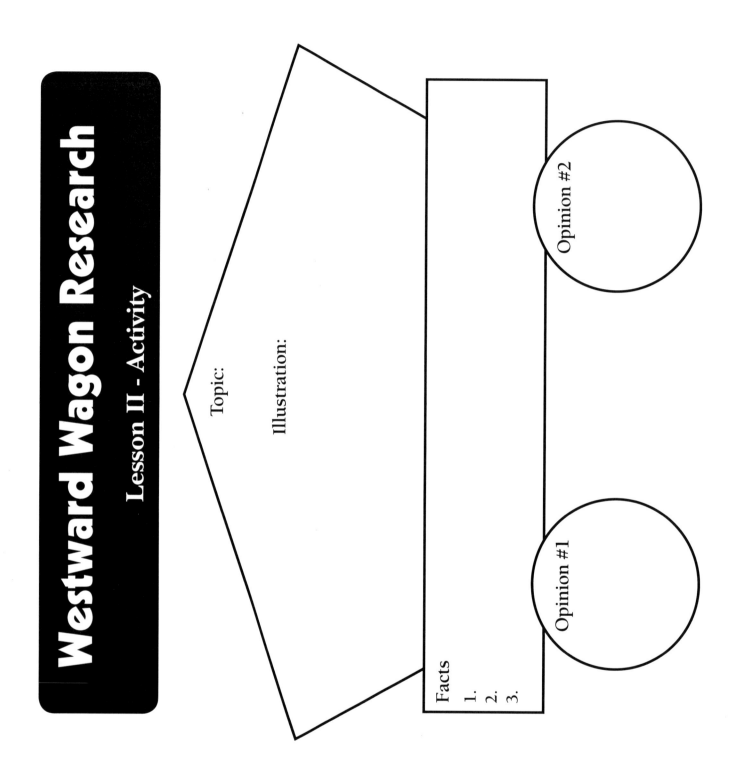

Topic:

Illustration:

Facts
1.
2.
3.

Opinion #1

Opinion #2

Famous Frontier Folks

Fact or Fiction?

It's true that some historical figures led such extraordinary lives that they seem legendary. It's also true that some literary characters have been so brilliantly written they seem to be real.

For example:

Christopher "Kit" Carson was fourteen when he left home to become an apprentice to a saddle maker. He ran away and became a frontiersman who had many adventures as an Indian Agent, Pioneer Scout, and Civil War Officer.

Francis Alphonse Tucket was fourteen when he was separated from his family who were traveling west on the Oregon Trail. He was captured by Indians, escaped with the help of a trapper, and had many adventures as he tried to reunite with his family.

Kit Carson, the famous frontiersman, was a **factual** person.

Francis Tucker appears in Gary Paulsen's book, *Mr. Tucket.* He is a **fictional** character.

Do you think these "characters" are fact or fiction?

Billy the Kid   Calamity Jane

Caddie Woodlawn   Febold Feboldson

Famous Frontier Folks

Fact or Fiction?

Directions: Match the "frontier folks" to the correct description.

1. _____ Paul Bunyan

2. _____ Buffalo Bill Cody

3. _____ Johnny Appleseed

4. _____ Davy Crocket

5. _____ Slue-foot Sue

6. _____ Pecos Bill

7. _____ Annie Oakley

8. _____ Daniel Boone

A. *Fact* – His real name was John Chapman and he planted apple orchards in Illinois, Indiana, Kentucky, Pennsylvania, and Ohio. (Two hundred years later, some of those trees still bear apples.)	**E.** *Fiction* – He was raised by coyotes when he fell out of his parents' covered wagon. It is said he could ride tornados and used a rattlesnake as a whip.
B. *Fact* – He cleared a trail through the Cumberland Gap, which is known as the "highway to the frontier."	**F.** *Fact* – A brave frontiersman, politician, and soldier, he is still considered "King of the Wild Frontier."
C. *Fact* – Born William Frederick Cody, this former army scout became the founder of the very popular Wild West Show.	**G.** *Fiction* – She was a remarkable cowgirl who was said to be able to ride a catfish down the Rio Grande River.
D. *Fiction* – This enormous man is said to have cleared the land in North Dakota and South Dakota and dug the Missouri River.	**H.** *Fact* – Know as "Little Sure Shot" she was the star sharpshooter of Buffalo Bill's Wild West Show.

Famous Frontier Folks

Fact or Fiction? Answer Key

Directions: Match the "frontier folks" to the correct description.

1. __D__ Paul Bunyan

2. __C__ Buffalo Bill Cody

3. __A__ Johnny Appleseed

4. __F__ Davy Crocket

5. __G__ Slue-foot Sue

6. __E__ Pecos Bill

7. __H__ Annie Oakley

8. __B__ Daniel Boone

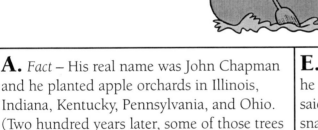

A. *Fact* – His real name was John Chapman and he planted apple orchards in Illinois, Indiana, Kentucky, Pennsylvania, and Ohio. (Two hundred years later, some of those trees still bear apples.)	**E.** *Fiction*– He was raised by coyotes when he fell out of his parents' covered wagon. It is said he could ride tornados and used a rattle-snake as a whip.
B. *Fact*– He cleared a trail through the Cumberland Gap, which is known as the "highway to the frontier."	**F.** *Fact*– A brave frontiersman, politician, and soldier, he is still considered "King of the Wild Frontier."
C. *Fact*– Born William Frederick Cody, this former army scout became the founder of the very popular Wild West Show.	**G.** *Fiction*– She was a remarkable cowgirl who was said to be able to ride a catfish down the Rio Grande River.
D. *Fiction*– This enormous man is said to have cleared the land in North Dakota and South Dakota and dug the Missouri River.	**H.** *Fact*– Know as "Little Sure Shot" she was the star sharpshooter of Buffalo Bill's Wild West Show.

Celebrate Earth Day!

• Library Lessons •

by | Lynne Farrell Stover

Grades 3–6

Earth Day was first celebrated in the United States on April 22, 1970. At this point in history, air pollution was so bad that people with breathing problems sometimes had to stay indoors, and certain rivers were so full of chemicals, they actually caught on fire. Created as a day to raise awareness of important environmental issues, Earth Day has developed into a global campaign addressing the need to protect our planet's precious resources and systems. This lesson invites cooperation with teachers in a cross-curricular unit.

Hoot Synopsis

Roy Eberhardt, a quick-witted, undersized middle-school student has just moved from mountainous Montana to flat Florida. Here he encounters the huge, slow-witted bully, Dana Matherson. While on the school bus, being tormented by Dana, Roy sees a shoeless boy his age running along the sidewalk. His curiosity is aroused and sets off a chain of events that connects Roy with Beatrice Leep and her runaway stepbrother, Mullet Fingers, and involves him in a guerilla warfare-style campaign to save the natural habitat of endangered burrowing miniature owls from the evils of an unscrupulous corporate restaurant chain. Students need not have read *Hoot* to successfully complete these lessons.

Lesson I (Reading): Hooray for Hoot! A Dramatic Story

Roy, the main character in *Hoot,* is a clever and compassionate young man. He knows that it will take drastic measures to save the habitat of a group of endangered owls. He also knows there is strength in numbers, and organizes a student protest at the construction site of a corrupt corporate fast-food restaurant. Give your students an opportunity to join Roy's protest. This short, but very popular, activity allows the "inner actor" in children to come out as they stomp feet, wave arms, and hiss like snakes. Note: This lesson works well as a component of a language arts or drama class.

Time Required: 15–20 minutes

Objective
Students will participate in an interactive, teacher narrated, dramatic story, based on the book *Hoot.*

Materials
*   copies of script "Hooray for Hoot!" on page 175
*   optional: copies of various environmental stories for students to check out and read (see suggested book list below)

Directions
1. Photocopy the script for all of your students.
2. Explain that the activity is based on the book *Hoot* by Carl Hiaasen. Clarify that the whole class must participate for the drama to be successful.
3. Pass out copies of the script and assign roles. In a small group all may participate; in a large class assign half the even number characters and the other half the odd numbers.

4. Review each character response with students. For example, say "Baby Owls" and have students respond with "heh-heh."

5. Read "Hooray for Hoot!" to the class, pausing at the bold print words for student response. If time allows, read the script twice. The first time as a rehearsal; the second the main event.

6. Encourage students to write their own dramatic plays.

Students interested in *Hoot* may also enjoy:

- *Adam Canfield of the Slash* by Michael Winerip. Candlewick Press, 2007.

- *Flush* by Carl Hiaasen. Knopf, 2007.

- *Hatchet* by Gary Paulsen. Simon & Schuster, 2007.

- *Holes* by Louis Sachar. Farrar, Straus and Giroux, 2008.

- *Maniac Magee* by Jerry Spinelli. Little, Brown and Company, 1999.

- *There's an Owl in the Shower* by Jean Craighead George. HarperCollins, 1997.

- *Whales on Stilts* by M. T. Anderson. Harcourt, 2005.

- *Who Really Killed Cock Robin?* by Jean Craighead George. HarperCollins, 1992.

Lesson 2 (Writing): Zippy Poems

Endangered animals can be found many places other than Carl Hiaasen's Florida. Students will enjoy writing a syllable-structured poems about animals based on the numbers found in specific ZIP codes. Note: This lesson works well as a component of a geography or science class.

Time Required: 25–35 minutes

Objectives

- Students will create a poem using a specific formula.

- Students will determine the number of syllables in words.

- Students will research information on the Internet.

Materials

- Zippy Poems visual (page 176)

- Zippy Poems activity sheet (page 177)

- writing tools

- optional: computers with Internet access

Directions

1. Prepare the visual and activity sheets prior to class. If specific zip codes are required, prepare a list of the places with their zip codes before class. The Web sites www.zip-codes.com and www.50states.com/zipcodes are user friendly.

2. Display the visual. Read and review it with the students.

3. Pass out the activity sheets. Students may use local zip codes they know, the zip codes listed on the visual, or zip codes of specific places they've located on the Internet, as you prefer.

4. Allow 10–15 minutes for students to complete the activity. They may share their poems with the class. The illustrated poems make an attractive bulletin board.

Lesson 3 (Research): Endangered Animal Tri-fold Task

The burrowing owl referred to in *Hoot* is, truly, protected as a Species of Special Concern. Students are often interested in animals that are endangered or extinct. A quick and easy research activity can stimulate curiosity while exercising those often underused encyclopedias. Note: This lesson works well as a component of a science or art class.

Time Required: 30–40 minutes

Objectives

- Students will use appropriate reference tools to research a specific topic.

- Students will follow a formatted pattern to create a report.

Materials

- visual or student copies of Endangered Animal Tri-fold Task instruction sheet (page 178)

- reference tools—encyclopedias, science reference books, or Internet sites

- plain white paper, writing tools, and markers or colored pencils

Directions

1. Introduce the lesson by asking students if they understand the concepts of "endangered" and "extinct" species. (Endangered species are plants or animals whose ability to survive and reproduce has been put at risk by human activities. An extinct species no longer exists anywhere on Earth.) Explain that the plot of *Hoot* centers on saving an endangered animal—the burrowing owl.

2. Tell students they will create a brochure featuring an endangered animal.

3. Display and review the instruction sheet on page 178.

4. Ask students to choose an endangered animal they would like to save from extinction. They will use reference sources to learn about their animal and create an illustrated tri-fold brochure about it.

5. Pass out a piece of plain white paper to each student. Demonstrate how to fold the paper in three parts.

6. Encourage students to use the specific reference tool of your choice—encyclopedia, science reference books, or Internet sites. Students may choose an animal on their own or select one from the list at the end of this lesson.

7. These Web sites are good sources of information: www.kidsplanet.org/factsheets/map.html, www.earthsendangered.com/index.asp, www.worldwildlife.org/endangered/index.cfm.

8. Encourage students to share their finished brochures with the class.

Endangered Animals A-Z

Armadillo
Burrowing Owl
Cheetah
Dolphin
Elephant
Giraffe
Humpback Whale
Iberian Lynx
Jaguar
Kangaroo
Lemur
Mexican Wolf
Northern Spotted Owl

Ocelot
Peregrine Falcon
Quarry Worm Salamander
Rhinoceros
Snow Leopard
Tiger
Ultramarine Lorikeet
Venezuela Stubfoot Toad
Walrus
Xucaneb Robber Frog
Yak
Zebra

Hooray for Hoot!

A Dramatic Story

Characters:

1. Baby Owls ("heh-heh")

2. Parent Owls ("kssh-kssh" while

   flapping arms)

3. Roy: ("Call me Tex")

4. Protestors: (stomp feet)

5. Mullet Fingers: ("Save the Owls!")

6. Curly: ("What Owls?")

7. Pancake House: ("Yum-Yum")

8. Snakes: ("Hiss")

It was a beautiful day in sunny Florida. Protestors gathered around the construction site of a soon-to-be-built pancake house. Roy was worried. How could he prove that the pancake house was being built over the nests of some endangered burrowing owls? Would Roy be able to save the baby owls and the parent owls from Curly, the cruel and greedy construction crew foreman?

Roy and the protestors soon had help. Mullet Fingers, a homeless boy with a big heart, did not want to see the baby owls homeless either. Mullet Fingers had a plan to keep Curly and his pancake house from destroying the natural habitat of the birds. The protestors, a reporter for the local newspaper, and a television crew were surprised to discover a boy inside the owls' burrow! It was Mullet Fingers, hoping that the parent owls would soon return to prove to the authorities that they did, indeed, have a nest in the ground. When the parent owls proved too shy to return, Mullet Fingers tried to keep the construction crew away with a pail full of snakes.

Curly discovered the snakes in the pail were not real when he chopped them into little pieces of plastic. Just as he was preparing to pull Mullet Fingers out of the burrow, the protestors joined hands and began to sing. Roy, singing with the protestors, looked up in the sky and saw one of the parent owls returning. As the parent owl landed on Mullet Fingers' head, photographers from the newspaper and television station took pictures. Roy, Mullet Fingers, and the protestors now had proof that there were baby owls in burrow nests at the construction site. They were heroes! And Curly and the owners of the pancake house were in big trouble for trying to harm the burrowing owl, a protected species.

Zippy Poems

The zip code we use on letters and packages is a routing code developed by the United States Postal Service to help get the mail to its destination in a quick and efficient manner. ZIP is an acronym for the Zone Improvement Plan. The basic zip code consists of five numbers.

Directions for writing a **Zippy Poem**

Discover the zip code for a town or city whose name contains the name of an endangered animal. Think of words and phrases that describe that animal. Write a poem so that the syllables in each line match the corresponding number in the zip code. (Note: Zeros count as 10.) Be sure to include the animal's name in the poem, create a title, and include the name of the location and its zip code.

Example:

"Seals Swimming in the Sea"

Seal Harbor, Maine—04675

0	Swimming seals—mammals living in the sea
4	Over the waves
6	Under the cold water
7	Returning to land simply
5	To sleep in the sun.

Examples of locations with animal names:

Big Bear Lake, California—92315	Lynx, Ohio—45650
Bison, Oklahoma—73720	Otter Creek, Florida—32683
Dolphin, Virginia—23843	Owls Head, Maine—04854
Falcon Heights, Texas—28342	Seal Rock, Oregon—97376
Fisher, Louisiana—71426	Turtle Creek, West Virginia—25203
Fox Island, Washington—98333	Wolf, Wyoming—82844

Zippy Poems

A zip code used on a letter or package is the routing code used by the United States Postal Service. ZIP is an acronym for Zone Improvement Plan. The word zip implies that the mail travels faster when a zip code is used. The basic zip code consists of five numbers.

Can you think of a place named for an animal? Do you know its zip code? If not, you can find it at the Web site www.zip-codes.com. Write the ZIP code vertically. Think of words and phrases that describe the animal in the town's name. Write your poem so that the syllables in each line match the corresponding zip code number. (Note: Zeros count as 10.) Be sure to include the animal's name in the poem, create a title, and include the name of the location and its zip code. Illustrate your poem if you have time and be prepared to share your creation with the class.

Zippy Poem

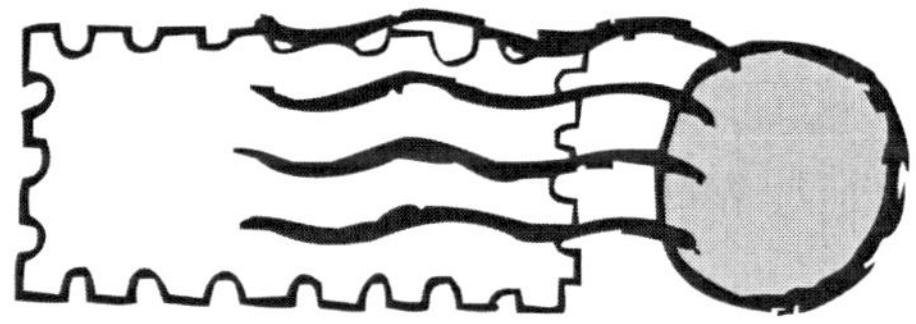

Title: _____

Place and Zip Code: _____

○

○

○

○

○

Endangered Animal Tri-fold Task

Choose an endangered animal and create your own tri-fold using the format in the example below.

Outside Tri-fold

Fun Fact Reference, Information Sources, Title and Illustration

The Barking Tree Frog

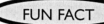 FUN FACT

This frog got its name because it has a deep bellowing voice that sounds like an old hound dog barking.

Information Sources

http://allaboutfrogs.org/info/species/barking.html

Tri-fold Prepared by:

Name:

Grade:

Teacher:

The Barking Tree Frog

A Special Animal

Inside Tri-fold

Three Interesting Facts

FACT I

The barking tree frog is the largest native tree frog in the southeastern part of the United States. They are about two inches long.

FACT II

Barking tree frogs have round toe pads that enable them to climb vertically on such things as tree trunks, fences, walls and windows.

FACT III

These frogs are good for pest control because they eat insects and other invertebrates.

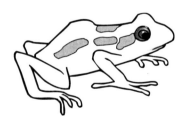

Guys Read & Succeed Club • Library Lessons •

by | Karen Larsen **Grades 3–6**

You need to be a reader to be a smart consumer and an intelligent citizen. To help boys, we need to realize they have a different take on reading.

—Jon Scieszka

According to Michael W. Smith and Jeffrey D. Wilhelm in *Reading Don't Fix No Chevys: Literacy in the Lives of Young Men* (Heinemann Library, 2002):

- Boys take longer to learn to read than girls do.

- Boys read less than girls read.

- Girls tend to comprehend narrative texts and most expository texts significantly better than boys do.

- Boys value reading as an activity less than girls do.

What can we do as educators to make sure that boys are successful in acquiring the lifelong habit and skills of reading? How can we motivate the reluctant male reader?

School librarians are in a unique position to collaborate with classroom teachers and public librarians to impact struggling male readers in positive ways. There are several methods for helping boys get on the road to reading. The "Guys Read and Succeed Club" is a fun and flexible program that works well as a summer reading program (with a summer commitment from you) or an in-house library program during the school year. You'll find program materials at the end of this lesson.

Suggested Procedure

1. Meet with classroom teachers and identify boys who might most benefit from this program. A small group of six to eight boys is ideal.

2. Contact the parents and tell them about the group. Make sure you have parent support, since some out-of-school time is involved.

3. If the boys don't have access to a public library or if you're doing the program in house, adapt the packet of materials on pages 181–185 to reflect that. If you're not meeting during the summer, remove references to summer reading programs at the public library.

4. Invite the boys to the library and tell them about the club. Snacks are a nice touch!

5. Give them their packets. Go over the contents as well as how to earn raffle prizes. Tickets are earned for showing up, for being on time, for being prepared, for making a positive contribution to the group, for completing out-of-class assignments, etc.

6. Go to a discount store and get prizes your boys would like. For example, you can get a set of ten superhero pencils for one dollar.

7. Work your way through the packet with the boys.

8. If you're doing an in-school club, have students help you set up table displays of books about each week's topic. Get their input about other books they would like to read about that topic and show them how you identify and order books. Let them help you order a few books for each topic. When the books come in, let them be the first to check them out.

9. Invite the boys to give booktalks related to the current topic to a class.

10. Write notes or make phone calls home acknowledging significant effort or progress.

11. Hold a raffle for small prizes each time you meet. Tickets are easy to make using any labels program. Let winners choose from the prizes you have stocked. You may want to incorporate a quick lesson on good sportsmanship as it relates to program rewards and recognition. Remind the boys that tickets carry over each time, so if they do not win on one day, they still have chances the next time.

12. Invite male administrators, teachers, fathers of the boys, or local leaders in for one of the sessions. Have them share their reading journeys. What books did they enjoy as children? What role does reading play in their lives now?

13. In one of your last sessions, have the boys make lists of books they want to read after the club is over. It's also interesting to have them share thoughts about what teachers could do to help boys get excited about reading.

14. When you start a new session of the Guys Read and Succeed Club, invite former members back to act as leaders or guests.

Suggested Resources

- *Boys Adrift: The Five Factors Driving the Growing Epidemic of Unmotivated Boys and Underachieving Young Men* by Leonard Sax. Basic Books, 2009.

- *Boys and Girls Learn Differently! A Guide for Teachers and Parents* by Michael Gurian. John Wiley & Sons, 2002.

- *Gotcha for Guys! Nonfiction Books to Get Boys Excited About Reading* by Kathleen A. Baxter and Marcia Agness Kochel. Libraries Unlimited, 2008.

- *Guys Write for Guys Read: Boys' Favorite Authors Write About Being Boys* by Jon Scieszka. Viking, 2008.

- *The Minds of Boys: Saving Our Sons From Falling Behind in School and Life* by Michael Gurian and Kathy Stevens. John Wiley & Sons, 2005.

- *Reading, Writing and Gender: Instructional Strategies and Classroom Activities that Work for Girls and Boys* by Gail Lynn Goldberg and Barbara Sherr Roswell. Eye on Education, Inc., 2002.

- *What Stories Does My Son Need? A Guide to Books and Movies that Build Character in Boys* by Michael Gurian. Penguin, 2000.

- *The Wonder of Boys: What Parents, Mentors and Educators Can Do to Shape Boys into Exceptional Men* by Michael Gurian. Penguin, 2006.

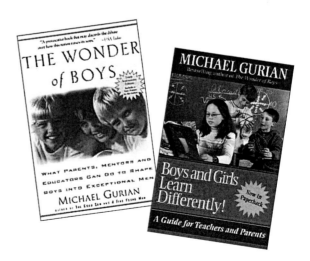

Guys Read and Succeed Club

Welcome to the Guys Read and Succeed Club! We are going to have a great time reading, writing, learning about all kinds of cool things, and earning fabulous prizes—yes, PRIZES!

You will earn raffle tickets for attending, for being on time, for participating during meetings, for completing activities, and for being a productive member of the group. We will have regular prize drawings. The more tickets you earn, the more prizes you could win.

In this packet, you will find activities that are fun and exciting to do. Complete the activities and win raffle tickets for the drawings.

If you have any questions, you can e-mail me at

_____.

Please bring this packet to our first meeting on

_____.

Remember to be on time.

I CAN'T WAIT!

→ ACTIVITY FOR WEEK ONE

Go to the public library and get a library card if you do not already have one. Sign up for the Summer Reading Program at the library while you are there. Go into the Youth Section and introduce yourself to the librarian at the desk. Tell her or him that you have a school assignment to have a short tour of the youth section of the library.

Signature of youth librarian _____

Date _____

After your tour, select three books to take home. Take some time to choose books that are interesting to you, and not too easy or too hard for you to read.

Complete the following:

Dear _____(Your club sponsor),

I went to the public library and took a tour of the Youth Section. While there I learned:

_____

_____

_____

_____

_____

The books I checked out were: (include the author's name)

_____

_____

_____

_____

_____

_____

My favorite book is _____

because _____

_____

_____

_____

THIS PAGE IS WORTH 5 RAFFLE TICKETS.

→ ACTIVITY FOR WEEK TWO

SPORTS!

What is your favorite sport? _____

Go to the library and check out at least one nonfiction book about this sport and at least one fiction book about this sport. In the nonfiction area, look in the 793–799 range for books about sports. Matt Christopher is a great author for books about sports. Look in the fiction section under CHR for his books. Ask the librarian for help if you need it. Remember to turn in your reading minutes to win prizes in the library's Summer Reading program!

My nonfiction book is: _____

by _____

My fiction book is: _____

by _____

Read both of your books and answer the questions below using complete sentences.

1. How were the books alike? _____

   _____

   _____

   _____

   _____

2. How were the books different? _____

   _____

   _____

   _____

   _____

3. Which book did you like better, and why?

   _____

   _____

   _____

   _____

   _____

THIS PAGE IS WORTH 5 RAFFLE TICKETS.

LEARN A NEW SKILL!

It's always fun to learn a new skill. Go to the library and browse the 791–796 area of the nonfiction section. You will find books on how to juggle, do yo-yo tricks, make cards or origami, do skateboard tricks, or try your hand at other great arts and crafts.

Choose a book, read it, and practice the skill. Be prepared to share your new talent when our group meets next on _____. Don't forget to turn in your reading minutes while you are there and earn prizes from the library!

My book is: _____

by _____

With a parent, get on the Internet. In an appropriate search engine (www.google.com for example), type in "How to _____" (juggle, do a magic trick, etc.) Find a Web site that tells you more about your new skill.

Name of Web site: _____

What information did you find on this site? Describe at least three things you learned from the site. Use your best handwriting.

_____

_____

_____

_____

_____

_____

_____

_____

_____

What advice would you give someone who is learning this skill?

_____

_____

_____

_____

_____

THIS PAGE IS WORTH 5 RAFFLE TICKETS.

ALL ABOUT ANIMALS!

What is your favorite wild animal? _____

What is your favorite domestic (pet or farm) animal? _____

Go to the library and look in the 590s for wild animals and in the 636s for pets and farm animals. Choose one book from each section. Then have the librarian help you find a fiction book about animals at your reading level.

My book about wild animals is: _____

by _____

My domestic animal book is: _____

by _____

My fiction animal book is: _____

by _____

Which of the three books do you like best, and why?

_____
_____
_____
_____
_____

On another piece of paper, write a fiction or a nonfiction story about an animal. Use your best handwriting. Draw a picture of each of the animals you studied. Bring both to your next club meeting on _____.

Draw a picture of each of the animals you studied.

THIS PAGE IS WORTH 5 RAFFLE TICKETS.

Summer Exploration Stations

• Library Lessons •

by | Pat Miller Grades 3–5

Whether you end your school year in May, as most Texas districts do, or continue into the middle of June, the last weeks of the school year are hectic. Fixed schedules are often anything but as we try to squeeze in field days, last field trips, award assemblies, end of year parties, yearbook signings, the last choir program, PTA/PTO programs, and perhaps even a last book fair. Therefore, the idea of teaching library skills in this maelstrom is more reasonable if we use our time to review what we taught through the year.

End the year with your intermediate grade students by setting up some summer exploration stations to review the Dewey Decimal system, feature some lesser known books, and encourage thoughts of summer reading.

Catalog Search Version

The simplest way to review the Dewey Decimal system and your collection is to give students a list of the Dewey divisions and have them search your automated catalog for titles that fit each and relate to summer. Before you begin, brainstorm with them what they could search for, including summer activi- ties, summer foods, summer poems, etc. You might conduct the activity as a scavenger hunt, awarding points and prizes for correct answers.

DEWEY	TITLE
000 Computer Science, Information, and General Works	
100 Philosophy and Psychology	
200 Religion	
300 Social Sciences	
400 Language	
500 Science	
600 Technology	
700 Arts & Recreation	
800 Literature	
900 History and Geography	
B Biography	

Exploration Station Version

If you have more time and want to implement exploration stations, follow these steps:

1. Select the books you want for each Dewey section. Use the chart on page 188 to give you ideas of books to use from your own collection.

2. Set up an activity area for each Dewey hundreds category. Include only those areas for which you have chosen books. Make paired signs from card stock that indicate the Dewey number. Tape them together so they form a pocket with the numbers or letters facing out. Slip the pocket over a bookend. This will identify the seating or floor area.

3. Make and/or duplicate activity slips for each station, and place copies near each Dewey sign. Or put all of the questions on a student handout and duplicate for each child. See activity slips on pages 188–191 for suggestions based on books in the recommended book list. They should work, with some modification, for similar titles in your collection.

4. Put the appropriate books, activity slips, or handouts at each station.

5. To assign students to stations, laminate card stock on which two or three of each Dewey number you're using is printed; enough to give each child one number as a starting point. To save cutting and laminating, simply write the numbers with permanent marker on the design side of a pack of playing cards.

6. Have students rotate through the stations from the point where they begin to the highest number, and then to the lowest Dewey number and up until they reach their starting points.

Prizes for completing a minimum number of stations could include bookmarks (see the sample below) or possibly coupons to a local pizza place, ice cream parlor, or fun children's place. If local businesses don't have their own coupons, ask if they would authorize and honor one you design and print, like 10% off, one free scoop when you buy another, etc. Happy end of the year, happy summer, and, most of all, happy reading!

Summer Reading Lists Abound on the Web!

www.educationworld.com/a_curr/curr244.shtml

Dewey Hundreds	Dewey Number	Suggested Titles
000	004.67	*Internet Safety* by Josepha Sherman. Children's Press, 2003.
100		
200	299	*Hawaiian Myths of Earth, Sea, and Sky* by Vivian Laubach Thompson. University of Hawaii Press, 1988.
300	394.263	*The Summer Solstice* by Ellen B. Jackson. Millbrook Press, 2003.
400	428.1	*A to Z Summer* by Tracy Maurer. Rourke Press, 2003.
500	508.2	*Hot Days* by Jennifer S. Burke. Scholastic Library Publishing, 2000.
	508.2	*The Nature and Science of Summer* by Jane Burton. Gareth Stevens, 1999.
	508.2	*Summer: Signs of the Season around North America* by Valerie J. Gerard. Picture Window Books, 2002.
600	639.2	*Salmon Summer* by Bruce McMillan. Houghton Mifflin, 1998.
	641.8	*Ice Cream Treats: The Inside Scoop* by Paul Fleisher. Carolrhoda Books, 2000.
700	745.5	*Crafts to Make in the Summer* by Kathy Ross. Lerner Publishing Group, 1999.
	782.4	*Camp Granada: Sing-Along Camp Songs* by Frane Lessac. Henry Holt & Co., 2003.
	790.1	*The Kids Summer Games Book* by Jane Drake. Kids Can Press, 1998.
	790.1	*38 Ways to Entertain Your Parents on Summer Vacation* by Dette Hunter. Firefly Books, 2005.
	793.73	*Summer: An Alphabet Acrostic* by Steven Schnur. Houghton Mifflin, 2001.
	796.48	*100 Unforgettable Moments in the Summer Olympics* by Bob Italia. Abdo Publishing, 1996.
800	811	*Lemonade Sun: And Other Summer Poems* by Rebecca Kai Dotlich. Boyds Mills Press, 2001.
	811	*The Night Before Summer Vacation* by Natasha Wing. Grosset & Dunlap, 2002.
	811	*Summersaults: Poems and Paintings* by Douglas Florian. Greenwillow Books, 2002.
	821	*Hot Like Fire: Poems* by Valerie Bloom. Bloomsbury Publishing, 2009.
900	938	*Spend the Day in Ancient Greece: Projects and Activities that Bring the Past to Life* by Linda Honan. Wiley, 1998.
	973	*Americana Adventure* by Michael Garland. Penguin Group, 2008.
B		Biographies are a stretch for this activity, but you might select any that are related to summer activities, like visiting a Disney theme park or eating ice cream.
		Ben and Jerry: Ice Cream for Everyone by Keith Elliot Greenberg. Sagebrush Education Resources, 1999.
		Walt Disney: Meet the Cartoonist by Carin T. Ford. Enslow Publishers, 2003.

Exploration Station Activity Cards

name: _____

Library Section: 200 Religion

Before scientists knew what causes summer days to be longer and hotter, people invented stories to tell the reasons. Read one of these and give the reason found in the story.

name: _____

Library Section: 300 Social Sciences

Many celebrations occur in the summer months of June, July, and August. What are two of them? Tell one thing people do to celebrate each.

1. _____

2. _____

Name: _____

Library Section: 600 Technology

Summer is a great time to find out how fish are caught or ice cream is made. You can go on a field trip, or read a book like the ones in this station.

Tell two interesting facts you learned about how people do things in these books.

1. _____

2. _____

Name: _____

Library Section: 700 Arts and Recreation

Summer is a great time to play a sport, learn a skill, start a hobby or make a craft. Using the book(s) in this station, find a craft or summer sport that looks interesting to you. Tell what the craft or sport is and why it interests you.

Name: _____

Library Section: 400 Language

Look at the summer activities listed in your book(s). Spell your name so the first letter is on the next line, the second letter below it, and so on. Then use each letter for a summer action.

Name	Actions

Use the back for more letters of your name if needed.

Name: _____

Library Section: 500 Science

What is nature (trees, weather, flowers, animals) doing that tells you summer is here? Name three things from your books.

1. _____

2. _____

3. _____

name: _____

Library Section: B (Biography)

Many of the things you enjoy in the summer, or the places you visit, were invented or established by people. Skim the biographies in the center to tell what the person made that you could do or use in the summer.

1. _____

2. _____

---

name: _____

Library Section: _____

Library Section: 800 Literature

Find a summer poem you like and share it with your group. Write a sentence to tell what the poem was about. Write another sentence to tell why you liked this poem.

name: _____

---

name: _____

Library Section: 900 History and Geography

If you were in Ancient Greece during the summer, what two things would you choose to do?

1. _____

2. _____

Summer Reading for Fall Success

• Library Lessons •

by | Karen Larsen

Grades K–2, 3–5

I would be most content if my children grew up to be the kind of people who think decorating consists mostly of building enough bookshelves.

—Anna Quindlen, "Enough Bookshelves," *The New York Times*, 7 August 1991

In addition to being able to use the bathroom anytime I want, my favorite thing about summer is sitting out on my deck with a tall glass of iced tea and a good book. Unfortunately not all of our students daydream about summer reading. Many of our students manage to survive the entire summer without reading a single book.

For those children who choose not to read over the summer, the consequences can be huge. In these days of high-stakes testing, any loss of academic achievement can hurt not only the child, but the entire school as well. According to a recent study by Harris Cooper, a professor of Psychological Sciences at the University of Missouri, the average loss equals about one month on a grade-level equivalent scale. For low-income children, the news is even worse. On average, children from low-income families lose nearly three months of grade-level equivalency during the summer each year, compared to an average of one month lost by middle-income children when reading and math performance are combined. Another study found that all young people experience learning losses when they do not engage in educational activities during the summer. In fact, students typically score lower on standardized tests at the end of summer vacation than they do on the same tests at the beginning.

Fortunately, this is where the school librarian can come to the rescue. By implementing a school-wide summer reading program, you can create an atmosphere of success for all students. Studies show that children who read as little as six books over the summer maintain the level of reading skills they achieved during the preceding school year. Reading more books leads to greater success. When children are provided with ten to twenty self-selected children's books at the end of the regular school year, as many as fifty percent not only maintain their skills, but also actually make reading gains. The school librarian facilitates this success.

Summer Reading Kick Off

Here's a plan for launching a winning summer reading program:

1. Discuss the research surrounding student achievement and summer reading at a staff meeting. Share your plans for a summer reading kick-off.

2. Make enough copies of each reading list on pages 195–200 for each student in the school to have the appropriate list. Use a different color paper for each grade level. Levels correspond to the grade students will enter next fall.

3. Staple the Summer Reading Sheet on page 194 on top of each list and have teachers send these home at the end of school.

4. Meet with students. Booktalk great summer reads. Invite the Youth Services Librarian from the public library to visit and promote their summer reading program. Many bookstores also sponsor summer reading programs. Share flyers about those programs with your students, too.

5. Have teachers from the next grade level visit with their incoming students to discuss their requirements or expectations for participating in the summer reading program.

6. Set a realistic goal of a certain number of forms to be returned the first week of school. Have a school-wide silent reading party as a prize if the goal is achieved.

7. Get donations for prizes. Everyone who turns in a form will win a small prize, and the names will be entered into a drawing for larger prizes. Recruit your parent organization to help obtain and distribute prizes.

8. Have the principal make announcements each day for the last week of school to talk up the summer reading program.

9. Pair up grade levels to visit the library at the same time. Have older students show younger students books they enjoyed during this school year.

10. Parental involvement is critical to the success of the program. Be sure to inform and involve parents via the school newsletter and post information along with the reading lists on the school Web site. Include a reminder about the summer reading program with the school letter that is sent to parents in August.

11. Give away donated books at the end of the school year so that children who may not be able to get to a public library have books to read over the summer.

12. In the fall, celebrate with all your summer readers.

References Concerning Achievement Loss Over Summer

• Booth, Alan and J. F. Dunn. Schools and Children at Risk. Family-School Links: How Do They Affect Educational Outcomes? (pp. 67-89). Lawrence Erlbaum, 1996.

• Borman, G. D. and M. Boulay. Can a Multiyear Summer Program Prevent the Accumulation of Summer Learning Losses? Summer Learning: Research, Policies, and Programs. Lawrence Erlbaum, 2004.

• Borman, G. D. (2001). Summers Are for Learning. Principal, 80(3), 26-29.

• Cooper, H., Nye, B., Charlton, K., Lindsay, J., and Greathouse, S (1996). The Effects of Summer Vacation on Achievement Test Scores: A Narrative and Meta-analytic Review. Review of Educational Research, 66(3), 227-268. rer.sagepub.com/content/vol66/issue3, keyword search.

• Mraz, Maryann and Timothy V. Rasinski. Summer Reading Loss. www.readingrockets.org/article/15218.

• Roderick, M., M. Engel, and J. Nagaoka. Ending Social Promotion: Results from Summer Bridge. Consortium on Chicago School Research, 2003. ccsr.uchicago.edu/content/publications.php?pub_id=22.

• Schacter, J. Reducing Social Inequality in Elementary School Reading Achievement: Establishing Summer Literacy Camps for Disadvantaged Children. Milken Family Foundation, 2003. www.mff.org/publications/publications.taf?page=297.

Summer Reading Sheet

Student Name: _____ Grade: _____

Set a Goal! How many books do you plan to read this summer? _____

Please keep track of the books you read or that are read to you over the summer. Bring in this completed sheet at the beginning of the school year and collect a prize! You do not need to fill up every line to win a prize. Just use this form to keep track of what you have read this summer.

Parents/Guardians: Research has shown that students who do not read over the summer can lose one to three months of progress in reading. Students who do read over the summer and have involved parental support with reading can actually gain achievement in reading. Please send this completed form back with your child on the first day of school. Be sure to check out the summer reading program at our local public library!

Books Read in June		
Title/Author	Read Alone	Read To

Books Read in July		
Title/Author	Read Alone	Read To

Books Read in August		
Title/Author	Read Alone	Read To

Parent/Guardian Signature: _____

Kindergarten Suggested Summer Reading List

Note: The following books are only suggestions. Please feel free to add any books that are appropriate for your reader. The staff in the children's area of the public library will also have many wonderful recommendations for you.

Research has shown that the single greatest factor in predicting reading success is whether a child is read to when young. Here are some titles to get you started! Please note that the reading levels vary. If your child is already reading, have him or her read a page of the book aloud to you to see if it is a good fit. If your child struggles with more than a few words on the page, it may be too difficult for independent reading, but would still be a great book to read aloud.

Books About Me
- *I Like Me!* by Nancy L. Carlson. Puffin, 2009.
- *I Like to Be Little* by Charlotte Zolotow. HarperCollins, 1990.
- *The Mixed-Up Chameleon* by Eric Carle. HarperCollins, 1998.
- *My Five Senses* by Aliki. HarperFestival, 1991.
- *Owen* by Kevin Henkes. Greenwillow Books, 1993.
- *When I Get Bigger* by Mercer Mayer. Random House, 1999.

Family Stories
- Just Me Books by Mercer Mayer from Random House.
- *Mama Do You Love Me?* by Barbara M. Joosse. Storytime, 1993.

Predictable Books
(Stories with a pattern using rhyme or rhythm.)
- *Curious George* by H. A. Rey. Houghton Mifflin, 1973.
- *Each Peach Pear Plum* by Janet and Allan Ahlberg. Puffin, 1986.
- *The Gingerbread Boy* by Paul Galdone. Houghton Mifflin, 1993.
- *Gregory the Terrible Eater* by Mitchell Sharmat. Scholastic, 2009.
- *Goodnight Moon* by Margaret Wise Brown. HarperCollins, 2005.
- *If You Give a Pig a Pancake* by Laura Joffe Numeroff. Harper Collins, 2000.
- *Millions of Cats* by Wanda Gág. Puffin, 2006.

Beginning, Middle, and End Concept
- *A Camping Spree with Mr. Magee* by Chris Van Dusen. Chronicle, 2003.
- *Daddy Goes to Work* by Jabari Asim. Little, Brown and Co., 2006.
- *Love You Forever* by Robert Munsch. Firefly Books, 1995.
- *Rosie's Walk* by Pat Hutchins. Aladdin, 1971.
- *The Runaway Bunny* by Margaret Wise Brown. HarperCollins, 2005.
- *That's Not Right* by Alan Durant. Crabtree, 2004.

Color and Counting Books
- *Each Orange Had 8 Slices: A Counting Book* by Paul Giganti Jr.. Greenwillow Books, 1992.
- *Fish Eyes: A Book You Can Count On* by Lois Ehlert. Sandpiper, 1992.
- *Inch by Inch* by Leo Lionni. Knopf, 2010.
- *Is it Red? Is it Yellow? Is it Blue?* by Tana Hoban. Greenwillow Books, 1987.
- *One is a Snail, Ten is a Crab: A Counting by Feet Book* by April Pulley Sayre. Candlewick Press, 2006.
- *One Leaf Rides the Wind* by Celeste Mannis. Puffin, 2005.
- *Planting a Rainbow* by Lois Ehlert. Houghton Mifflin Harcourt, 2008.
- *Ten Little Fish* by Audrey Wood. Blue Sky Press, 2004.
- *26 Letters and 99 Cents* by Tana Hoban. Mulberry Books, 1995.

Caldecott Winners and Honor Books
- *Color Zoo* by Lois Ehlert. HarperCollins, 1989.
- *Madeline* by Ludwig Bemelmans. Viking, 2000.
- *More, More, More Said the Baby* by Vera B. Williams. Greenwillow Books, 1996.
- *Officer Buckle and Gloria* by Peggy Rathman. Putnam, 1995.
- *Swimmy* by Leo Lionni. Knopf, 1973.
- *Tops and Bottoms* by Janet Stevens. Harcourt, 1995.

Mother Goose and Nursery Rhymes
- *James Marshall's Mother Goose* by James Marshall. Square Fish, 2009.
- *My Very First Mother Goose* by Iona Opie and Rosemary Wells. Candlewick Press, 1996.
- *Tomie de Paola's Mother Goose* by Tomie de Paola. Putnam, 1985.

Folktales and Fairy Tales
- *Chicken Little* by Steven Kellogg. HarperCollins, 1987.
- *Cinderella* by Marcia Brown. Aladdin, 1997.
- *The Hare and the Tortoise* by Brian Wildsmith. Oxford University Press, 2007.
- *Henny Penny* by Vivian French. Bloomsbury, 2006.
- *The Little Red Hen* by Margot Zemach. Farrar, Straus and Giroux, 1993.
- *The Three Bears* by Paul Galdone. Sandpiper, 1985.
- *The Three Billy Goats Gruff* by Peter Christen Asbjornsen. Tambourine, 1995.
- *Three Little Pigs* by James Marshall. Grosset and Dunlap, 2000.
- *The Three Little Pigs* by Rodney Peppé. Lothrop Lee & Shepard, 1980.
- *The Ugly Duckling* by Hans Christian Andersen, illustrated by Jerry Pinkney. HarperCollins, 1999.

Stories in Rhyme
- *All the Colors of the Earth* by Sheila Hamanaka. Mulberry Books, 1999.
- *Bringing the Rain to Kapiti Plain* by Verna Aardema. Puffin, 1992.
- *Miss Spider's Tea Party* by David Kirk. Scholastic, 2007.

Friends
- *George and Martha* by James Marshall. Houghton Mifflin, 1987.
- *We Are Best Friends* by Aliki. Mulberry Books, 1987.
- *Who Will Be My Friends?* by Syd Hoff. HarperCollins, 1985.

Fabulous Science Books
- *Growing Frogs* by Vivian French. Candlwick Press, 2003.
- *Magic School Bus On the Ocean Floor* by Joanna Cole. Scholastic, 1994.
- *What Do Wheels Do All Day?* by April Jones Prince. Houghton Mifflin, 2006.

First Grade Suggested Summer Reading List

Note: The following books are only suggestions. Please feel free to add any books that are appropriate for your reader. The staff in the children's area of the public library will also have many wonderful recommendations for you.

Research has shown that the single greatest factor in predicting reading success is whether a child is read to when young. Here are some titles to get you started! Please note that the reading levels vary. If your child is already reading, have him or her read a page of the book aloud to you to see if it is a good fit. If your child struggles with more than a few words on the page, it may be too difficult for independent reading, but would still be a great book to read aloud.

Fun Books to Share
- *Adventures of Morris the Moose* by Bernard Wiseman. Barnes and Noble, 2005.
- *And I Mean It, Stanley* by Crosby Bonsall. HarperCollins, 1984.
- Arthur series by Marc Brown from Little, Brown and Co.
- *A Bad Case of the Stripes* by David Shannon. Scholastic, 2004.
- Berenstain Bear series by Jan and Stan Berenstain from Random House.
- Clifford series by Norman Bridwell from Scholastic.
- *Dinosaur Time* by Peggy Parish. HarperCollins, 1983.
- *The Eye Book* by Theo LeSieg. Random House, 1999.
- Franklin series by Paulette Bourgeois from Kids Can Press.
- Froggy series by Jonathan London from Puffin Books.
- *Green Eggs and Ham* by Dr. Seuss. Random House, 2007.
- *Hi! Fly Guy* by Tedd Arnold. Cartwheel Books, 2006.
- *How I Became a Pirate* by Melinda Long. Harcourt, 2003.
- Junie B. Jones series by Barbara Park from Random House.
- Little Critter series by Mercer Mayer from Random House.
- Nate the Great series by Marjorie Weinman Sharmat from Delacorte.
- *Rainbow Fish* by Marcus Pfister. North-South Books, 1995.
- *The Very Busy Spider* by Eric Carle. Philomel, 1989.

Learning to Read Series
- Hello Reader! from Scholastic, Inc.
- I Can Read Books from HarperCollins.
- Puffin Easy-to-Read
- Step Into Reading Levels 1–4 from Random House.

Alphabet Books
- *Animalia* by Graeme Baese. Puffin, 1996.
- *The Icky Bug Alphabet Book* by Jerry Pallotta. Charlesbridge, 1993.
- *Z Was Zapped* by Chris Van Allsburg. Houghton Mifflin, 1987.

Math in Picture Books
- *The Great Graph Contest* by Loreen Leedy. Holiday House, 2006.
- *How Much Is a Million?* by David M. Schwartz. Harper Trophy, 1997.
- *Ten Sly Piranhas: A Counting Story in Reverse (A Tale of Wickedness—and Worse!)* by William Wise. Puffin, 2004.
- *When Sheep Cannot Sleep* by Satoshi Kitamura. Farrar, Straus and Giroux, 1988.

Classics to Read to a First Grader
- *Leo the Late Bloomer* by Robert Kraus. HarperCollins, 1994.
- *The Little House* by Virginia Lee Burton. Houghton Mifflin, 1978.
- *Make Way for Ducklings* by Robert McCloskey. Viking, 1941.
- *When Will I Read?* by Miriam Cohen. Greenwillow Books, 1977.

Caldecott Awards and Honor Books
- *Alphabet City* by Stephen Johnson. Puffin, 1999.
- *Ashanti to Zulu: African Traditions* by Margaret Musgrove. Puffin, 1992.
- *The Hello, Goodbye Window* by Norton Juster and Chris Raschka. Hyperion, 2005.
- *Owen* by Kevin Henkes. Greenwillow Books, 1993.
- *A Story, A Story* by Gail E. Haley. Aladdin, 1998.
- *What Do You Do With a Tail Like This?* by Steve Jenkins. Houghton Mifflin, 2008.

Enjoy!

Second Grade Suggested Summer Reading List

Note: The following books are only suggestions. Please feel free to add any books that are appropriate for your reader. The staff in the children's area of the public library will also have many wonderful recommendations for you.

Research has shown that the single greatest factor in predicting reading success is whether a child is read to when young. Here are some titles to get you started! Please note that the reading levels vary. If your child is already reading, have him or her read a page of the book aloud to you to see if it is a good fit. If your child struggles with more than a few words on the page, it may be too difficult for independent reading, but would still be a great book to read aloud.

School Stories
- *Amazing Grace* by Mary Hoffman. Dial, 1991.
- *Amelia Bedelia's First Day of School* by Herman Parish. Greenwillow Books, 2009.
- *The Day Jimmy's Boa Ate the Wash* by Trinka Hakes Noble. Puffin, 1992.
- *Fish Face* by Patricia Reilly Giff. Yearling, 1984.
- *Junie B. Jones* series by Barbara Park from Random House.
- *Lilly's Purple Plastic Purse* by Kevin Henkes. Greenwillow Books, 1996.
- *Miss Nelson Is Missing* by Harry Allard. Sandpiper, 2007.
- Kids of Polk Street School series by Patricia Reilly Giff from Yearling.

Books about Friends
- *A Bargain for Frances* by Russell Hoban. HarperCollins, 1992.
- *Fox on the Job* by James Marshall. Puffin, 1995.
- *Frog and Toad Together* by Arnold Lobel. HarperFestival, 1999.
- *Horrible Harry and the Green Slime* by Suzy Kline. Puffin, 1998.
- *My Best Friend* by Mary Ann Rodman. Puffin, 2007.
- *Pinky and Rex* by James Howe. Simon Spotlight, 1998.

Historical Fiction
- *Kamishibai Man* by Allen Say. Houghton Mifflin, 2005.
- *Players in Pigtails* by Shana Corey. Scholastic, 2006.
- *The Several Lives of Orphan Jack* by Sarah Ellis. Groundwood Books, 2005.

Classics to Read Aloud
- *Alice in Wonderland* by Lewis Carroll. CreateSpace, 2010.
- *Charlotte's Web* by E. B. White. HarperCollins, 2001.
- *Just-so Stories* by Rudyard Kipling. General Books, 2010.
- *A Bear Called Paddington* by Michael Bond. Houghton Mifflin, 2008.
- *Winnie the Pooh* by A. A. Milne. Dutton, 2009.

Caldecott Awards and Honor Books
- *The Funny Little Woman* by Arlene Mosel. Puffin, 1993.
- *Many Moons* by James Thurber. Sandpiper, 1998.
- *The Ox-Cart Man* by Donald Hall. Viking, 1979.
- *The Story of Jumping Mouse* by John Steptoe. HarperCollins, 1989.

- *Sylvester and the Magic Pebble* by William Steig. Simon & Schuster, 2005.
- *When I Was Young in the Mountains* by Cynthia Rylant. Puffin, 1993.

Learning to Read Stories
- Berenstain Bears series by Jan and Stan Berenstain from Random House.
- Young Cam Jansen series by David A. Adler from Puffin.
- Hello Reader! from Scholastic, Inc.
- I Can Read Books from HarperCollins.
- Junie B. Jones series by Barbara Park from Random House.
- Puffin Easy-to-Read
- Step Into Reading Levels 1–4 from Random House.
- *The Stories Julian Tells* by Ann Cameron. Random House, 1989.

Enjoy!

Third Grade Suggested Summer Reading List

Note: The following books are only suggestions. Please feel free to add any books that are appropriate for your reader. The staff in the children's area of the public library will also have many wonderful recommendations for you.

Research has shown that the single greatest factor in predicting reading success is whether a child is read to when young. Here are some titles to get you started! Please note that the reading levels vary. If your child is already reading, have him or her read a page of the book aloud to you to see if it is a good fit. If your child struggles with more than a few words on the page, it may be too difficult for independent reading, but would still be a great book to read aloud.

School Stories
- *Gooney Bird Greene* by Lois Lowry. Houghton Mifflin, 2004.
- *Jake Drake, Teacher's Pet* by Andrew Clements. Atheneum, 2007.
- *Kirsten Learns a Lesson: A School Story* by Janet Beeler Shaw. The Pleasant Company, 1986.
- *Ramona Quimby Age 8* by Beverly Cleary. Avon, 1992.

Animal Stories
- The Paddington Bear series by Michael Bond from Houghton Mifflin.
- *Babe: The Gallant Pig* by Dick King-Smith. Knopf, 2005.
- *Catwings* by Ursula K. Le Guin. Scholastic, 2003.
- *Mr. Popper's Penguins* by Richard and Florence Atwater. Little, Brown and Co., 1992.
- *Rats on the Roof and Other Stories* by James Marshall. Puffin, 1997.

Books about Friends
- *The Candy Corn Contest* by Patricia Reilly Giff. Yearling, 1987.
- *Pinky and Rex* by James Howe. Simon Spotlight, 1998.

Historical Fiction/Biography
- *Ben and Me: An Astonishing Life of Benjamin Franklin by His Good Mouse Amos* by Robert Lawson. Little, Brown and Co., 1998.
- *Changes for Addy* by Connie Rose Porter (and other American Girl books) from The Pleasant Company.
- *If You Grew Up with George Washington* by Ruth Belov Gross. Scholastic, 1993.
- *Kate Shelley and the Midnight Express* by Margaret K. Wetterrer. Live Oak Media, 1991.
- *Pink and Say* by Patricia Polacco. Philomel, 1994.
- *Snowflake Bentley* by Jacqueline Briggs Martin. Houghton Mifflin, 1998.
- *Teammates* by Peter Golenbock. Sandpiper, 1992.

Folktales
- *The Girl Who Loved Wild Horses* by Paul Goble. Atheneum, 2001.
- *Kibitzers and Fools: Tales My Zayda Told Me* by Simms Taback. Viking, 2005.
- *Mirandy and Brother Wind* by Patricia C. McKissack. Dragonfly Books, 1997.

- *Raven: A Trickster Tale from the Northwest* by Gerald McDermott. Sandpiper, 2001.
- *The Talking Eggs* by Robert D. San Souci. Dial, 1989.

Great Series Books
- Amelia Bedelia series by Peggy Parish from Greenwillow Books.
- American Girl series from The Pleasant Company.
- Arthur series by Marc Brown from Little, Brown and Co.
- Berenstain Bears series by Jan and Stan Berenstain from Random House.
- Boxcar Children by Gertrude Chandler Warner from Albert Whitman.
- Encyclopedia Brown by Donald J. Sobol from Puffin.
- Eyewitness Science Explorers from DK.
- Henry and Mudge series by Cynthia Rylant from Atheneum.
- Horrible Harry series by Suzy Kline from Puffin.
- Little House series by Laura Ingalls Wilder from HarperCollins.
- Nancy Drew Notebooks by Carolyn Keene early series from Aladdin.
- Pee Wee Scouts by Judy Delton from Random House.
- Polk Street School by Patricia Reilly Giff from Yearling.

Award Winners
- *Actual Size* by Steve Jenkins. Houghton Mifflin, 2004.
- *The Cat Who Went to Heaven* by Elizabeth Jane Coatsworth. Aladdin, 2008.
- *Doctor De Soto* by William Steig. Square Fish, 2010.
- *Jumanji* by Chris Van Allsburg. Houghton Mifflin, 1981.
- *Mercy Watson to the Rescue* by Kate DiCamillo. Candlewick, 2009.
- *Mirette on the High Wire* by Emily Arnold McCully. Putnam, 1997.
- *Prehistoric Pinkerton* by Steven Kellogg. Puffin, 2002.
- *Rabbit Hill* by Robert Lawson. Puffin, 2007.
- *Show Way* by Jacqueline Woodson. Putnam, 2005.
- *The Village of Round and Square Houses* by Ann Grifalconi. Little, Brown and Co., 1986.

Enjoy!

Fourth Grade Suggested Summer Reading List

Note: The following books are only suggestions. Please feel free to add any books that are appropriate for your reader. The staff in the children's area of the public library will also have many wonderful recommendations for you.

Research has shown that the single greatest factor in predicting reading success is whether a child is read to when young. Here are some titles to get you started! Please note that the reading levels vary. If your child is already reading, have him or her read a page of the book aloud to you to see if it is a good fit. If your child struggles with more than a few words on the page, it may be too difficult for independent reading, but would still be a great book to read aloud.

School Stories
- *Frindle* by Andrew Clements. Atheneum, 1998.
- *Harriet, the Spy* by Louise Fitzhugh. Yearling, 2001.
- *My Teacher Fried My Brains* by Bruce Coville. Aladdin, 2005.
- *Ramona and Her Father* by Beverley Cleary. HarperCollins, 2001.
- *Sideways Stories from Wayside School* by Louis Sachar. HarperCollins, 2004.

Mystery and Adventure Stories
- *Cam Jansen and the Mystery of the UFO* by David Adler. Puffin, 1997.
- *The Castle in the Attic* by Elizabeth Winthrop. Yearling, 1994. (A challenging independent read)
- *Encyclopedia Brown Gets His Man* by Donald J. Sobol. Puffin, 2007.
- *Julian, Secret Agent* by Ann Cameron. Random House, 1988.

Sports Stories
- *Baseball Fever* by Johanna Hurwitz. HarperCollins, 2000.
- *Bobby Baseball* by Robert Kimmel Smith. Yearling, 1991.
- *The Mayor of Central Park* by Avi. HarperCollins, 2005.
- *Soccer Cats: Switch Play* by Matt Christopher. Little, Brown and Co., 2003.
- *Swimming with Sharks* by Betty Hicks. Roaring Brook, 2008.
- *Three on Three* by Eric Walters. Orca Books, 1999.

Historical Fiction
- *The Hundred Penny Box* by Sharon Bell Mathis. Puffin, 2006.
- *Little House in the Big Woods* by Laura Ingalls Wilder. HarperFestival, 2005.
- *The Well* by Mildred D. Taylor. Puffin, 1998. (A challenging independent read)
- *The 13th Floor: A Ghost Story* by Sid Fleischman. Greenwillow Books, 2007.

Fantasy and Science Fiction
- *Aliens Ate My Homework* by Bruce Coville. Aladdin, 2007.
- *The Lion, the Witch, and the Wardrobe* by C. S. Lewis. HarperCollins, 2009. (A challenging independent read)

Series Books
- Animal Planet Extreme Animals from the Discovery Channel
- The Baby-Sitter's Club by Ann M. Martin from Scholastic.
- The Boxcar Children by Gertrude Chandler Warner from Albert Whitman.
- Cam Jansen by David A. Adler from Puffin.
- Goosebumps by R. L. Stine from Scholastic.
- The Hardy Boys by Franklin W. Dixon from Grosset & Dunlap.
- Harry Potter by J. K. Rowling from Scholastic.
- Marvin Redpost series by Louis Sachar from Random House.
- Nancy Drew Mysteries by Carolyn Keene from Aladdin.
- A Series of Unfortunate Events by Lemony Snicket from HarperCollins.

Enjoy!

Fifth Grade Suggested Summer Reading List

Note: The following books are only suggestions. Please feel free to add any books that are appropriate for your reader. The staff in the children's area of the public library will also have many wonderful recommendations for you.

Research has shown that the single greatest factor in predicting reading success is whether a child is read to when young. Here are some titles to get you started! Please note that the reading levels vary. If your child is already reading, have him or her read a page of the book aloud to you to see if it is a good fit. If your child struggles with more than a few words on the page, it may be too difficult for independent reading, but would still be a great book to read aloud.

Great Reads
- *Black Stallion* by Walter Farley. Yearling, 1991. (A challenging independent read)
- *From the Mixed-Up Files of Mrs. Basil E. Frankweiler* by E. L. Konigsberg. Atheneum, 2007.
- *Granny Torrelli Makes Soup* by Sharon Creech. HarperCollins, 2005.
- *Hatchet* by Gary Paulsen. Simon & Schuster, 2007.
- *Holes* by Louis Sachar. Farrar, Straus and Giroux, 2008.
- *Maniac Magee* by Jerry Spinelli. Little, Brown and Co., 1999.
- *Mick Harte Was Here* by Barbara Park. Yearling, 1996.
- *Wringer* by Jerry Spinelli. HarperCollins, 2004.

Mystery and Adventure
- *Island of the Blue Dolphins* by Scott O'Dell. Sandpiper, 2010.
- *The True Confessions of Charlotte Doyle* by Avi. HarperCollins, 2004. (A challenging independent read)

Newbery Medal and Honor Books
- *Afternoon of the Elves* by Janet Taylor Lisle. Putnam, 1999.
- *Catherine, Called Birdy* by Karen Cushman. Clarion Books, 1994.
- *Dragon's Gate* by Laurence Yep. HarperCollins, 1995. (A challenging independent read)
- *The Ear, the Eye, and the Arm* by Nancy Farmer. Firebird, 2002.
- *Homesick, My Own Story* by Jean Fritz. Dell, 1987.
- *Missing May* by Cynthia Rylant. Scholastic, 2004.
- *The Watsons Go to Birmingham* by Christopher Paul Curtis. Laurel Leaf, 2000.

Historical Fiction
- *Bull Run* by Paul Fleischman. HarperCollins, 1995.
- *Code Talker: A Novel About the Navajo Marines of World War Two* by Joseph Bruchac. Dial, 2005.
- *Number the Stars* by Lois Lowry. Houghton Mifflin, 1989.
- *Sarah Bishop* by Scott O'Dell. Houghton Mifflin, 1992.

Fantasy and Science Fiction
- *The BFG* by Roald Dahl. Puffin, 2007.
- Harry Potter series by J. K. Rowling from Scholastic.
- *The High King* by Lloyd Alexander. Henry Holt, 2006. (A very challenging independent read)

- *The Lion, the Witch, and the Wardrobe* by C. S. Lewis. HarperCollins, 2009.
- *Over Sea, Under Stone* by Susan Cooper. Margaret K. McElderry Books, 2007.
- *Redwall* by Brian Jacques. Philomel, 2002. (A challenging independent read)
- *A Wrinkle in Time* by Madeleine L'Engle. Square Fish, 2007.

Humorous Stories
- *Freaky Friday* by Mary Rodgers. HarperCollins, 2003.
- *Matilda* by Roald Dahl. Puffin, 2007.
- *Skinnybones* by Barbara Park. Yearling, 1997.

Enjoy!